1

This book is lovingly dedicated to Lana – my wife, partner, friend, confidant, counselor, navigator, and planner. I can't imagine life without her.

Table of Contents

FORWARD

It could never be said that I am a Biblical scholar. I am fairly knowledgeable, in broad terms of Scripture, I heard stories in Sunday School as a kid, listened to more sermons on God's word than I could possibly count, have read the Bible through many times, and spend time almost every day reading and studying God's word. I have learned a great deal about God's nature and his characteristics from Scripture over the years. I would say that I know just enough to know how little I really know.

In the past several years I have run headlong into an inescapable fact about God's nature. This particular trait of God's is found throughout the Bible in many circumstances across many centuries. But, experience had shown this characteristic trait to me as well. He tends to use the unexpected, the unlikely, and even the almost impossible to show himself and to accomplish amazing things.

Scripture is full of men and women who were anything but the obvious choices in the eyes of other people, but yet God chose them to do his work, and often miraculous things. There was a comparison that was common on social media a few years back that listed some of the unlikely folks that God used, and that effectively illustrates the trait of God using the unlikely:

> Noah was a drunk
> Abraham was too old
> Isaac was a dreamer
> Jacob was a liar
> Leah was ugly
> Joseph was abused
> Moses had a stuttering problem
> Gideon was afraid
> Samson had long hair and was a womanizer
> Rahab was a prostitute
> Jeremiah and Timothy were too young
> David had an affair and was a murderer

Elijah was suicidal
Isaiah preached naked
Jonah ran from God
Naomi was a widow
Job went bankrupt
Peter denied Christ
Three Disciples fell asleep while praying
Martha worried about everything
The Samaritan woman was divorced
Zacchaeus was too short
Paul was too religious
Timothy had an ulcer
Lazarus was <u>dead</u>.

And this is just a partial list of the God's unlikely choices in Scripture. But all of these people were, in fact chosen by God to do amazing things.

Likewise, I am sure that many of us have seen God in places where we did not expect to find him: perhaps in the classroom, at work, in the grocery store, even in a prison. And while we have all heard of such things, or even encountered them, we are usually still unprepared to encounter them, and are usually caught off-guard when God shows up when and where we least expect him.

In short, God has a tendency for the unexpected and unusual; at least his choices seem so to most people. So, it should have come as no real surprise when I very clearly and unmistakably saw God and his love through an old bus.

CHAPTER 1

MY LITTLE GIRL

Where do I begin? Keri is my little girl. She will always be my little girl. She is the youngest of our three children. From the moment I held her in my arms in the delivery room the afternoon she was born, she had me wrapped around her little finger. Her two older brothers were great kids, and have grown up to be fine men of whom I am very proud and love without bounds. But my little girl has always been special to me. I have always felt that man was God's prototype, and woman was his perfected product. Anyway, you get the idea.

Fast forward to 2008. At the age of 22, Keri had completed a bachelor's degree and was accepted in grad school in Cincinnati to study to become a counselor. I recall chatting with her in our kitchen before she left for Cincinnati that fall. I told her of all of the times I had moved and the times that her mother (Lana) and I had moved. Through my experience, I advised her to find a church home as soon as she could. This would keep her rooted in her relationship with Jesus and help her to find community and support. Sure enough, very soon after moving she found a church home and became involved.

In November as I recall, I had an excited phone call from Keri. She had tried out for a part in her church's big Christmas outreach production and got the part. She was thrilled. Over the next few weeks, Lana and I made plans to travel to Cincinnati in mid-December to see the production, and to visit with Keri.

Then, I got the call - the call that no parent wants. The call that many parents have nightmares about. I remember very clearly that I was sitting in our family room alone watching TV. Lana had a night class and was on her way home. When the phone rang I answered to find that it was Keri's pastor. I tried to make small talk for a few seconds, just being friendly, when he said that this was a phone call that he wished he did not have to make. He told me that Keri had been in an accident while performing in the Christmas production that night, and had been taken to the hospital unconscious.

As soon as Lana got home, we headed for Cincinnati. Along the way, Lana slowly pieced together the grave nature of Keri's injuries. She solicited prayer from anyone she could reach on the phone. Then, she called the hospital to try to find out about Keri. The nurse told her that Keri had suffered a severe head injury and there was concern that there was no longer any brain function.

My world changed with that comment. My only response was "Not my little girl!"

After what seemed like forever, we finally arrived at the hospital and found several of the pastoral staff of Keri's church and a family friend with her. As the night wore on, we learned that Keri had no hope for recovery; she was already gone. We decided to remove life support. She drew her last breath that night as I held her hand.

The next few days are a blur of tears and details. During the days following Keri's death, we received literally thousands of cards and letters from people we knew, and even people we didn't know all offering their sympathy and support. One note in particular stood out to me. I don't even recall who sent it to me. The note explained that when a person loses his/her parents, they are called an orphan. If a man loses his wife, he is called a widower. Likewise, if a woman loses her husband, she is called a widower. These are all tragic losses. But it noted that losing a child is so horrible there is not even a word describing those left behind. This note helped me somehow in acknowledging how horrible and complete losing a child is.

As difficult as it was, I had to watch my two sons and my bride suffer the loss as well. The outpouring of love from friends and family was the one thing that saw me through those dark days. Several days later as we were packing up Keri's things and cleaning out her apartment, I found a coffee mug in her kitchen that carried the words "Friends are God's way of taking care of us". I have no doubt that God used these people to comfort us.

THE NEW NORMAL

The weeks and months after Keri died were very dark for me. Lana seemed to bear the loss better than I did at first. After all of our family left, I went back to work, and we both tried to make sense of our loss. As the days turned into weeks and months I noticed Lana slipping further and further away. The encouraging words she had for me right after Keri's death had turned into frequent sobs and sleepless nights for her. She struggled to get through each day. She seldom left the house, unable even to go to church. And all I could do was to watch her suffering grow deeper and deeper, while I struggled to deal with my own loss. This was our "new normal". It was not what we wanted or liked, but it was what we had to live with and deal with.

I was blessed to have had many friends call or simply drop by to "chat" and show love and support. I spent many hours with friends over a meal or cup of coffee talking through what happened and how I was doing. It was comforting to know that people cared, but I still had to go home and watch Lana suffer and grieve. It seemed like the world had closed in on me and was getting darker and darker.

I knew of several friends who had lost children. The massive loss they had experienced had become all too real for me, and I began to understand how calloused and unsupportive I had been to them at the time of their losses. I had deemed their losses as any other loss through death: bad albeit, but that was life. That was the way things go. Now I understood all too well.

During those first months, I reached out to several of these friends, knowing that we now had something in common – they had all lost children - and I wanted to try to learn from their experiences. I needed help to find my way out of this tunnel. One of the pastors at our church had lost his three year old daughter several years before. So, I contacted him and asked if we could meet and chat. So, one day I left work a little before noon and met him at a local coffee shop.

Over the course of three to four hours we talked. He told me about his daughter and his loss, and I shared with him about Keri. As heart-breaking as his experience was, it was reassuring to me in a way that he had gone through the same tunnel I was in and had somehow managed to get through it. Not that he had "gotten over it" or ever would, but he had gotten through it. But he shared one thing with me that proved to be the most profound thing I heard during this dark time. He said that as incredibly difficult as it was to lose his daughter, it was just as difficult to watch his bride suffer and grieve knowing that there was absolutely nothing he could do to help her. My ears heard his words, but they didn't really sink in for a few more months.

As, night after night, week after week I watched my beautiful and vibrant bride struggle just to get through each day, and then struggle to get through each night, and watched her active and fulfilling life seemingly ebb away, the pastor's words became all too real. It broke my heart all over again to watch Lana suffer knowing that there was nothing I could do to help her. It would be up to God whether or not she would get through this, and if so when.

LIFE GOES ON

One of the most surprising revelations for me as I dealt with the incalculable loss of my precious daughter was the fact that the rest of the world carried on like nothing had happened. Didn't they realize that one of God's most beautiful creations had died, and that her family was suffering greatly? How could they go to work, carry on small talk, laugh, like nothing had happened?

What was happening was that life went on, and so it does. Life continues no matter what has happened to any of us. But that was not exactly the case for my family, as it is with the family of anyone who has suffered such a loss. However, we had to press ahead as well as we could. Our lives, too would go on. We just weren't sure what they would be like.

I returned to work, although I was not able to be very productive or focused. Lana also returned to work. We did our best to live our lives, horribly altered though they were. Part of this life was to at least think about retiring in the ever-closer future. We had discussed retirement in vague terms throughout our married life, but never any real concrete plans. We had been blessed financially, and had done prudent financial planning, but had no real definitive time frame for either of us to retire.

Lana's parents had both retired early for a variety of reasons, at about age 55. Shortly thereafter, they purchased a small travel trailer and began taking trips in it and the Chevy Suburban they pulled it with. Over time both the travel trailer and the Chevy grew, eventually becoming a big fifth-wheel and a diesel "dually" pickup truck. Now, properly equipped they became official snowbirds, spending several winters in south Texas. They enjoyed it so much that they eventually sold their house, stored their household belongings and became full time RV-ers for several years.

Back to our retirement planning and discussions. Over the years Lana had mentioned that she would possibly like to move to someplace warmer, as that would be much easier on her physically. But, I had no desire to live in the land of "blue hair". Plus, the advent of grandchildren just a couple of miles away removed from both of us all desire to move. So, we eventually compromised and decided that we might could spend some of the colder months in a warmer climate, renting a place to stay. If we liked it there, we could return in subsequent years. If not, we could try someplace new for our next winter. We had not made firm retirement plans; we had just shared our preferences about retirement. With no definite plan, this was where our retirement discussions ended.

During subsequent discussions (*not necessarily about retirement*) Lana mentioned that she would enjoy taking RV trips with her parents. Never having traveled in an RV and not owning a truck I politely acknowledged her desire and promptly dismissed it to the "I'll think about it later" file.

CHAPTER 2

THE ADVENTURE BEGINS

In the spring of 2012 I began to feel that it was time for me to retire. I had been blessed with a career I enjoyed, with great employers and places to work, and very capable and supportive people to work with. But, Keri's death had left me with little passion for my work. Things at work left me with the impression that my effectiveness had passed and that I was no longer able to make a significant contribution to the success of my employer.

So, I sought out advice from men I respected: my father-in-law and a good friend with whom I had been involved in a prison ministry for several years. Both of these men had been retired for some time, and I knew that I could trust their input. Through multiple conversations with them both, I heard the same message regarding the timing of retirement: "You'll know when it's time". What? No bells? No FedEx delivery bearing a proclamation that it was time for me to hang it up? No tap on the shoulder? I will just know?

The more I thought about their comments, the more I realized that they were right, and that it was time for me to leave the world of the Social Security contributors and join the ranks of the Social Security check cashers.

So, not really knowing what I would do or how I would fare with not going to work every day as I had for the previous 35 years, I gave notice to my employer that I intended to retire at the end of the year. That November I packed up my office, said a few goodbyes and turned in my company ID badge and office key and drove home for the last time. It was not a profound or sad event. For me, it was just time.

The first few months were a bit of an adjustment, as it is for many when they retire. I enjoyed taking care of things that I had put off because I didn't have the time. One of these things was some serious planning and thinking: What now?

NEW MEMORIES

Memories are very powerful for most of us. Their recall can be triggered by a sound, a smell, an event or seeing something. I must admit that much of my teen years was spent listening to music. Now, when I hear one of the songs that were special to me "back in the day" played on the oldies station (*Yep. That's about the only place I can hear these songs now other than my trusty old 8 track tape player.*), I am instantly transported back in time, cruising the circuit in my hand-me-down 1961 Buick Le Sabre and singing along. And, yes, my brain is still clogged with the lyrics to most every song I ever heard.

Seriously, many of us have fond memories of the house we grew up in, a favorite teacher, our first car, our favorite aunt or uncle, and on and on. Reminiscing can bring these pleasant memories back to us allowing us, in some small way to relive these pleasant times.

Unfortunately, the same thing happens with unpleasant memories. We all have them. Some are relatively minor, like the time you got sent to the principal's office, the time the fancy cheese cake dumped upside down in the back seat of the car, or that first speeding ticket. But for most of us, some of these bad memories were burned into our consciences by tragic events. It seems that the more tragic the event, the more vivid and painful are the memories. Such was the case for my family with the death of Keri.

Soon after Keri died, Lana mentioned to me on several occasions how hard it was to continue to live in the house that Keri called home. The memories were just too real for her. Such was not the case for me. Actually, it was just the opposite for me. I took great comfort in living in the house that Keri called home. It maintained a connection to her for me. But Lana's pain was far greater than the comfort this afforded me. We did eventually move to another house. But our discussions brought me to realize how badly Lana needed to begin to allow the horrible memories to begin to fade and to make new, more pleasant ones.

We frequently discussed trying to find activities that we could both enjoy together – things that had no connection to Keri at all. We talked about it, but never found anything that we were both comfortable in doing and would enjoy. So, we each continued to deal with Keri's death in our own way, and continued to cultivate our own lives and activities.

I was involved in a prison ministry and in the music ministry at our church. I was also involved in a music ministry with a dear friend, frequently playing for other churches and groups, and sharing our stories of God's grace and care in our lives.

For Lana, she just worked - which she loved. She had no outside activities that she could bear to be involved in. She had been involved in a ministry for young women with Keri, but it was simply too difficult for her to resume now. But, one day our front doorbell rang. It was a neighbor and friend of Lana's. It seems that a group of ex-teachers got together every Monday morning to chat and share their lives and to play bridge. She absolutely insisted that Lana come with her. Lana explained that she did not know how to play bridge, and that it would be too difficult for her to get out and be around people. But our neighbor refused to take no for an answer. So, Lana went, and this wonderful group of ladies became her support group. And every Monday morning became an island of enjoyment and "normal" for Lana: something that had no connection with or memory of Keri. Through these ladies I began to see a spark of life in Lana.

Over these many months it became increasingly clear to me just how important it was for Lana to create new memories: memories that could not possibly tie back to Keri. I became convinced that if Lana remained where she was emotionally she was just fade away. So, I felt that I had to do something . . . but what?

OK. I'LL TAKE A LOOK.

Lana's comments that she would like to take some RV trips with her parents came back to mind. Although I had no idea when Lana was thinking of taking such trips, her parents weren't getting any younger. With their RV-ing days limited, it seemed that if we were going to take any trips with them, we had better get serious about it. I thought I should at least start investigating our options for RV-ing. I think that, deep-down I probably thought that once I understood the costs involved I could dissuade Lana from this notion altogether. Even though we had been blessed financially, our income had taken a dramatic downturn with my retirement and we had to be conscious of what we spent.

There was one major consideration for me as I began to look into this RV thing: I knew absolutely nothing about it. I didn't know what to look for in an RV, how to travel in an RV, how to care for and maintain an RV, how to live in an RV. I barely knew how to spell RV. One this was for sure: I would need a lot of help from somebody.

Since Lana's folks had a truck and a fifth-wheel that seemed like the logical place to start. After all, I respected and trusted them. If this was a good solution for them, it must be a good one for us as well. So, that was my focus . . . until I realized how much a pickup truck suitable for pulling a fifth-wheel would cost. I had never owned a pick-up truck (*Even though I was by birth a redneck, I never felt called to drive a redneck Cadillac.*). If we bought one, I would have to give up my car. Then there was the issue of where to park it. A truck would not fit into our garage, and would not be well suited to hauling music equipment in cold or wet weather as I frequently did. Plus, parking outside in a northern Ohio winter is not my idea of a good time. No sir. No way. A pickup truck simply did not seem to be the right type of wheels for me.

Then there was the cost of a fifth-wheel on top of the truck cost. Fifth-wheel RVs are like anything else: they come in a variety of sizes and prices. Buying new would have been my preference, but that was a pricey option. But, the price for a used fifth-wheel in very good shape with a floor plan that suited us was a much larger number that I was prepared for. When I totaled up the cost for a truck and fifth-wheel rig, smoke came out the back of my calculator (*yes, I still had a calculator and it did not have a lever that you pulled*). OK. Time to look for a plan B.

Fifth-wheel rigs were too pricey. Travel trailer rigs would likely provide insufficient living space, plus we would still have the expense and aggravation of a truck. That left motorhomes.

The internet has changed many things in our culture and lives. It is so easy to get almost any information that you need, if you have a bit of persistence and patience. Researching RV options and the opinions of those who have experience with each type is a perfect use of current search engine capabilities. So, Google and I got to work. I discovered that there are more types, sizes and configurations of motorhomes than I ever thought possible. I realized pretty quickly that "new" would be out of our price range, so I started looking at good used rigs.

My search led me to several online forums for RV-ers which, as I quickly learned were a good source for people's real-life experiences with various manufacturers, equipment type and configurations and general RV-ing. While most of the comments that I found were specific to manufactured motorhomes, I began to see comments about "converted coaches". I wasn't sure what they meant, so down that bunny trail I went.

I found several websites and social media groups dedicated to converted coaches. I quickly learned that these were almost all buses that had served their working lives hauling people from one place to another (*school buses, city buses, or long-haul transport buses*). While some of the coaches people mentioned were commercially converted from a bus into self-contained motorhomes (*some were even brand new buses that had never been outfitted with seats or other accommodations for hauling people*), most had been converted by their owners. They purchased a used bus after it had been retired from service, removed all of the people hauling amenities, and built their own motorhome design into the bus shell.

I found an almost universal opinion that the converted coaches or buses were much more durable and road-worthy than their manufactured motorhome cousins. The buses were designed and built to drive for hundreds of thousands of miles, while the manufactured motorhomes were built to drive a little and stay a long time, with their predominant qualities being the technical amenities and creature comforts (*LED lighting, multiple large flat screen TV's, exotic hardwoods, granite counter tops . . . well, you get the idea*).

That made perfect sense to me. I was not altogether interested in the latest gadgetry. I wanted something that would be comfortable to travel in and be reliable and safe on the road. So, Google and I got to work again. This time looking for converted coaches for sale. Over the course of two to three months I looked at just about every converted coach I could find, and finally had a rough list of features that I thought would work for us. I identified two that looked like they would fit our needs, appeared to be in good shape and were within our reach financially.

I began to think that this whole idea of RV-ing was not such a bad one after all. But, I had not mentioned any of this to my bride. Then one day I told her that I had been researching options to allow us to fulfill her desire to RV with her folks. I explained about the costs associated with the fifth-wheel approach, and what I had learned about motorhome options. Then I mentioned the "B" word: "bus". To say that she was uncertain is an understatement. She had that "yeah, whatever" look on her face. I explained that I had found two that might work for us; one in Indiana and the other in Virginia. That's about as far as our conversation went that day.

I couldn't put the bus idea out of my mind. I was convinced that if we were going to RV at all, this would be the best approach for us. I kept an eye on the listings for the two buses that I had found and eventually decided to contact the owners to find out a bit more. When I contacted the owner of my first choice I found that it had already been sold. Bummer. Undeterred I moved on to my second choice: a bus in Virginia.

The owner and I exchanged several emails, which led to a phone call or two. I was convinced. This was worth taking a serious look at. So, we re-convened the family discussion about buses. Lana still did not seem altogether enthusiastic about the idea. As we talked I learned that she did not think there would be enough room for the two of us in a bus. She didn't think the living space in a bus would work for us at all. But she finally relented and agreed to drive to Virginia the next weekend to take a look. Worst case, we would have a nice long weekend drive.

OH, YEAH. THIS'LL DO

The trip to Virginia was not necessarily noteworthy. It was just a 600 mile drive, with a hotel stay in the middle. As I recall, our conversations were not really about the bus, RV-ing, or anything related. We just chatted as we drove. But the fact that I knew absolutely nothing about what we were going to look at or about the whole RV thing was never far from my mind.

We arrived mid-morning, having spent the night along the way. We were met by the owner. He is an engineer and converted the bus himself, so he wanted to tell me all about every technical detail as soon as we arrived. We finally convinced him to let us take a look inside. I went in first and was looking around, when Lana came in. I will never forget the look on her face as she came up the steps into the bus, turned toward the rear of the bus and came up into the lounge area. With a big grin on her face, her only comment was "Oh, yeah. This'll do". She was convinced.

Well, we spent most of the day looking into every nook and cranny (*not sure what nooks and crannies are, but I am certain that I looked in some of them*), at every piece of equipment, every detail. The owner finally asked me, "Do you want to drive it?" I had never driven a bus in my life. The largest thing I had ever driven was a little dump truck during a summer job when I was in high school. And that was in a big gravel pit, far away from anyone or anything that I could hurt or damage if I hit them. And the owner wanted me to drive a 40 foot long bus in traffic around other people and buildings? "Sure", I replied. OK. So, I have made wiser, more thoroughly thought out decisions in my life. But, realistically if we were even considering buying this or any bus, I had better find out if I can drive it.

So, with my bride comfortably seated on one of the couches in the lounge and the owner/builder in the co-pilot seat we were off. He carefully talked me through every step and coached me through every maneuver. I was reminded of flight training and having an instructor seated beside me talking me through every maneuver and turn (*I later learned that the owner was a commercial pilot as well. So he truly was in the role of flight instructor in the bus that day.*). Anyway, we drove for a while down several sections of four lane road making several turns, when the owner told me, "We'd better turn around. Turn in here" as he pointed to a big home improvement store on our left. A flood of sarcastic, but sincerely concerned thoughts flooded through my mind:

"You want me to go in there? Are you nuts? In there with all of those cars and people? Down that little, narrow path better suited for motorcycles than cars, not to mention a 40 foot long bus? Do you realize that I have a grand total of about 5 minutes of driving time in this thing? I can see it all now: the bus gets away from me and we wreck 30 or 40 cars and crash into the front of the building doing millions of dollars of damage. Our insurance company cancels our coverage and then sues us. We lose in court and have to live in a tent in the woods and sell pencils on a street corner just to eat."

"OK", I replied. Once again I have made wiser choices in my years on this planet. But into the parking lot we went, driving through the little pathway next to the building and then successfully out the other side. Man, I felt like a pro. Those big rig drivers on the highway got nothin' on me. "Breaker, breaker 1-9. Make way for THE bus." OK. So, I got a little carried away. But I was encouraged that I really would be able to drive this thing if we bought it.

As we drove back home the next day, Lana and I chatted about the particulars of the bus we had seen, how we might use it and enjoy it. We even discussed some of the practical matters like where we could keep it when we weren't in it on a trip. The next week or so I investigated many of the details of ownership like insurance and what type of license I needed to drive a bus. We chatted about the financial details of purchasing and refurbishing the bus. We decided that this was indeed the bus for us, if we can get it at the right price.

Lana has always bought the vehicles in our family. She is the negotiator and loves the process of haggling with the seller. So, several days later she called the owner and got down to business. She set her price and the requirement that one mechanical issue had to be resolved as a condition of purchase. After many days and several more phone calls, we reached an agreement we could all live with. We were going to be bus owners!

ED AND ANKE

Great. We had decided to be bus owners and RV all over the place. Were we nuts? All I knew about this bus was that it was big, and I could barely drive it. And, although I don't ever recall discussing it with her specifically, I don't believe that Lana had much of a clue what we would need inside the bus, or how to live in an RV. Finding the right RV or bus was certainly important, but we would need some know-how, and lots of it.

Enter Ed and Anke. They were the builders and now sellers of our soon-to-be bus. We liked them from the start. They had owned and driven the bus for some 20 years, over much of the continental US. As Ed tells it, Anke decided that she wanted something bigger (*Seriously? Bigger than 40 feet?*), so they bought a 45 foot long monster of a motorhome and now had to find a new home for their first bus.

Ed is an engineer by degree and profession. He owned an industrial controls company. As he tells the story, "One day a fellow walked into my office and wanted my company worse than I did, so I let him have it." Thus began Ed's retirement.

Although he never told me what prompted him to do so, he bought a retired 1965 Silver Eagle bus that had served its working life as a Continental Trailways bus hauling paying passengers across the highways and bi-ways of Virginia. It had already had all of the passenger stuff removed, and some of the very basic steps had been taken to convert it into a livable motorhome by the time he bought it. Completing the conversion of his bus became his full time retirement job. He purchased a huge garage that had been an auto garage and body shop to complete his work in. I don't think that Ed ever truly finished his work on his bus, though. He always had something that he wanted to add or do a better way. In fact, he tinkered so much with his bus, that it was given the name "Big Toy". No doubt, it was, in fact Ed's big toy.

When we returned to Virginia to actually purchase the bus, Ed spent an entire day with me, showing me and explaining every little detail of the bus and how each system operated. We went over all of the major automotive and RV equipment, and what things I needed to do with each. He even had me to go hands-on with many of these tasks, talking me through each one to make sure that I knew how to do each task.

Aside from the bus itself, Ed was a fountain of knowledge about general RV stuff. For example, he suggested a couple of RV groups for us to affiliate with that had been very helpful to him. We discussed roadside service, and again, he was eager to provide his experiences and make suggestions. We talked about GPS systems, engine monitoring systems, and much more. In short, I can't imagine that I could have possibly gotten (*or retained*) any more information.

Anke is very gracious and unassuming. She was helpful from the first conversation we had with her. She had driven a school bus for several years (*and actually still did*), and so, was quite at home driving their bus. She had designed much of the interior of the bus. Through all of the years they had travelled in the bus, she had mastered all of the household things that were necessary for life on the road in a bus.

I gathered that Anke played the role of planner and navigator when they travelled in the bus. As such, she shared her experiences with what things to look out for when travelling in a bus. Her years of experience had also taught her that, when making reservations in an RV park, never tell them that you will be driving a bus, or how long it is. People tend to freak out when they hear the term "bus". Just tell them it is a motorhome: they feel comfortable with those. When asked the length, be vague; "Oh, I'm not sure. 35 feet or a little more I think." Nothing major, but very practical information.

We had no clue what we would need for the inside of the bus. Anke was great about sharing what she used for almost every conceivable household function, and why. Things like what kind of dishes travel well (*I didn't think that the same china we use at home would travel well*). You know. This kind of stuff that everyone who drives a motorhome or RV needs to know, but usually has to learn for themselves the hard way.

Ed and Anke turnout to be more than just the people who built the bus, or who sold it to us. They were mentors in a very real sense.

AND AWAY WE GO

In early April we flew back to Virginia, check in hand and bought the bus: OUR bus. As we pulled out of the garage and onto the highway, I could not help but see a mental image of the Partridge Family in their 1960's mod-painted bus. Here we were. All we were missing were the other fourteen people, the mod paint job, the music, and the TV cameras. OK. So, we aren't the Partridge Family. But we were now bus owners, too.

The trip home was one I will never forget. I was completely focused on driving a 40 foot bus and trying to learn about the various systems (*windshield wipers, lights, etc.*) as we drove. So, I don't recall much about conversations or anything else. I did notice right away that the steering seemed to have a lot of play in it. I had mentioned this to the previous owner during our test drive. He indicated that this was just the way a large bus feels. But it took a lot of concentration to keep the bus centered in our lane of traffic.

Our first night in the bus was spent in a Wal-Mart parking lot. It had gotten dark, and I was tired. Ed had mentioned to us that some Wal-Mart stores allow RV-ers to overnight in their parking lots. So, when we noticed a Wal-Mart sign we exited the highway. There were no trucks or other RVs in the parking lot, so I got permission from the store manager for us to stay the night. I recall Lana taking a picture of the Wal-Mart sign through the bus windshield and sending it to our oldest son, telling him where we were spending the night. She thought it was great. This elicited the first real smile I had seen on my bride's face for almost 5 years.

YOU BOUGHT A WHAT?

We had made tentative arrangements for an outdoor storage lot for the bus before we went to pick it up. So, when we arrived at home in the bus, we drove right to the lot, finalized the details for its storage and parked it. But we had not thought through how we would get from the storage lot to our house. It would be about a 5 mile walk, and neither of us was very excited about that possibility. So, Lana called a neighbor to come and pick us up; in fact the same neighbor who had dragged Lana to the Monday morning bridge group.

Our neighbor met us at the storage lot office. As Lana began to explain why we needed a ride, our neighbor asked in disbelief, "You bought a what?" No amount of explaining could really get the concept across to her.

A couple of weeks later, I had the bus in front of our house taking care of some minor repairs and small maintenance tasks. When up walked our neighbor, and out of the house came Lana. Lana gave her a tour of the bus, and then they sat in the lounge and chatted. Our neighbor finally really understood that we had, indeed bought a bus.

Over the weeks to follow many of Lana's Monday morning group toured the bus. Some were astounded, others seeming indifferent, while still others could not possibly imagine why anyone in their right mind would want to buy a 50 year old bus. From their perspective, and from that of virtually everyone else, this purchase was on the very fringe of sanity. But, none of these folks had buried a child. None of them understood the devastation that brings. None of them had a desperate need to create new memories with no connection to the past. None of them would ever understand, and I could not have cared less. This old bus carried my hopes that Lana would finally find a way to move forward. And, from the look in her eyes and the comments she made about this bus, I could tell that we were on the right track.

CHAPTER 3

GRACE

Through my years as a Christian and follower of Jesus, I had heard of the concept of grace, but it was just that: a distant and fuzzy concept. On a retreat weekend, I heard perhaps the most descriptive and concise definition of God's grace I have heard: "God's unmerited favor". Let that sink in for a minute. God's grace means that he does for us things for which we have no right to expect, do not deserve or could ever deserve. It is something that we did not earn, nor could we ever earn. It doesn't mean that God will necessarily keep bad things from happening to us or in our lives. It doesn't mean that he will answer our prayers as we expect, or even when we expect. But it does mean that often, when we least expect it he will show up and demonstrate his love for us in ways we could not have possibly imagined. Please do not confuse the concept of grace with the gospel of prosperity spewed by several prominent TV preachers. It doesn't mean that God will make us all rich, give us great jobs, and generally make our existence in this life luxurious. It simply means that in ways we won't expect or deserve God will show us his love for us.

We can all probably recall instances of when God showed his love to us or to others in amazing and undeserved ways. Scripture also is full of examples of God's grace – his unmerited favor toward people, both individually and collectively.

Sarah, Abraham's wife overheard an angel of the Lord talking to Abraham. He promised that within one year she and Abraham would have a son. She laughed at the mere suggestion that she could have a baby. She was over ninety years old. Plus, she had previously gotten impatient waiting on God to give them a son, and had arranged for her handmaid, Hagar to sleep with Abraham so she and Abraham would have a son that way. She certainly did not deserve God's favor; she did not think too much of God's plan. Yet, sure enough she became pregnant and gave birth to Isaac.

Moses was certainly an unlikely character. Here he was, an abandoned baby, raised in the lap of luxury, a murderer, and a fugitive. Nope, I don't see anything there that might be deserving of anyone's special favor, let alone God's. As a man with a speech impediment he certainly would not be most people's ideal choice for a spokesperson. But, that is exactly what God used him for. God blessed him as no other man, calling him friend and speaking with him face to face. Yes sir, that's a blessing.

The Hebrew people certainly did not do anything to deserve God's favor. God had chosen them as his special people, but it was not because of anything they had done. In fact, the Old Testament is filled with story after story of the Hebrews rebelling against God in many ways, even by forsaking him altogether and worshiping idols. Yet, time and time again God blessed and preserved the Hebrews.

Rahab was a prostitute, and certainly would not have been in my top ten list of most deserving folks. However, God blessed her with the chance to save her entire family when the Hebrews defeated and destroyed the town of Jericho.

And on and on. You get the idea.

I am sure that most of us have heard stories of people being healed after praying for that healing, or finding a job after being unemployed and at the end of their financial rope, and many other practical instances of God's grace. But sometimes he uses the unusual and unlikely to show his love for us. Sometimes we will see a single instance of his grace and be in awe when we recognize it as such.

But, sometimes he will shower us with his grace. Like a line from a popular worship song says: "If grace is an ocean, we're all sinking". Yeah, that kind of grace. Grace so overwhelming and undeniable and unexpected and unrelenting that we are driven to our knees and reduced to tears as we begin to get the tiniest glimpse of just how much God really loves us - just as we are. Not for we "might" be, but for who we are right here, right now.

His grace is not something that we deserve. It is not something that God owes us. Rather, it is a result of the almost unfathomable love that he has for us – his creation – his people. He loves us and, thus wants to show this love.

And, sometimes his undeniable and unexpected and unrelenting grace is shown through the unusual and unexpected, like a 50 year old bus. Such is the case with us and our old bus. Time and time again he has shown his grace and his love for us through our old bus.

Such grace never fails to humble me and, in some regards shame me. After all of the times I have experienced his grace firsthand, I should have come to expect and rely on it by now. But such is not necessarily the case. I am always ashamed and saddened by the fact that I never expect such outpourings of love and grace. I tend to turn to God for help with such trivial things as repairing a bus only after I have tried everything I know and still come up short. But even after such last minute pleas, his grace is still poured out on me, time and time again.

CHAPTER 4

TOO BIG FOR THE DRIVEWAY

W e decided to buy a bus. A real live, 40 foot long - you can't park it in the driveway or in the street or the neighbors will run you out of town – bus. We had the check and airline tickets in hand and were leaving in just a couple of days to buy the bus and drive it home. But, the reality set in with me: where will we keep it. This had to be determined and quickly.

I spoke with a friend who lives in a very rural area. He and his wife don't have a great deal of land, but they do have a place beside a storage barn where the bus might fit. He graciously offered to let us keep it there. Great. Problem solved. Well, maybe not. I began to feel that this would really be imposing on the generosity of friends. But we may not have a choice. Maybe we could keep it there for a little while, just until we find someplace better.

So, I thought I would drive out and look it over, to make sure that we could actually get a 40 foot bus back to the spot offered. Well, this option quickly vanished into the mists of reality. While it might have been possible to get a bus back there, it would a tight fit and tricky at best. Plus, as I discussed it further with my friend, I learned that any rain at all turns the path from the road into a muddy mire which would certainly be a problem for a 40,000 pound bus. So, it would have to be dry weather, and have been dry or quite a while before we could get the bus out or put it back into storage there.

OK. Scratch that option. But the clock was ticking. Where could we keep a bus?

As I drove home I prayed (*as I often do as I drive*), but this time with a bit of urgency in my tone. I saw this bus as a chance to help my bride make new memories and perhaps begin to move away from the overwhelming grief of losing Keri. It was my responsibility as her husband to help her in any way I could, and this bus seemed like the only way I had encountered since Keri died of helping Lana. But, if we had no place to keep it, then I would have to give up on this whole idea. My prayer grew into a plea as I drove home.

Having driven these roads countless times before I hardly noticed anything, barely even noticing the traffic I encountered. Then I drove by an outdoor storage lot. I had driven by it literally hundreds of times before and had hardly ever even given it notice. But, now I did notice it.

The lot is owned by a friend who also owns an auto body shop very close by. Without so much as a thought, I turned into the body shop parking lot. I wasn't too sure what I would say, or what I would hear. But here I was.

The lady who manages the front desk of the body shop and all of the administrative chores for the outdoor storage business has a desk in the very front of the body shop building. So, as soon as I walked through the door, she said hello and asked how she could help me. I explained that we hoped to buy a bus, but had nowhere to store it, and wondered if they had room in their storage lot. I can still see her smile in my mind's eye as she said that yes, they did have a spot. Someone had just cancelled their spot. But, the location would be a bit challenging, especially for a 40 foot bus.

I asked her if I could go take a look at the spot. She agreed and gave me an access code for the gate. The available spot was situated so the bus could be pulled straight into an empty and never-to-be-used vacant corner of the lot and then backed into the available space. No other space in the lot would accommodate a 40 foot bus without partially or mostly blocking the path in and out for other storage customers.

I drove back to the office and sealed the deal for renting the available spot. Problem solved. However, it was not until several weeks later that I recognized God's hand – his grace – in this.

WHO'S GONNA FIX IT?

Let me get this out of the way right up front: I am no diesel mechanic. I am an engineer by degree, and a compulsive tinkerer. I have no fear in taking something apart to see how it works, or tackling the repair of most anything found around the house. But the working end of a 40 foot diesel bus was WAY outside of my comfort zone, and certainly beyond what I was willing to try. Plus, we did not have a facility that would accommodate extended work on a diesel engine or other related mechanical components, much less the necessary tools. So, it was essential that I find some way – or someone – to perform the necessary mechanical service.

When we got the bus home, I knew from the previous owner that it was just about due an oil change for both the primary engine and the onboard generator (*both large diesels*). The only oil changes I had ever done were on the family car using four quarts of oil. But, there was no way I could manage a 10 gallon oil change. I had no idea who even worked on this kind of stuff. I had never had the need for this type of work before, nor did I know anyone who had. Lana and I had tentatively planned to take our first trip in about 60 days, so I knew that I needed to get this work done, and pretty soon. We had several other refurbishing tasks that we wanted to get done, so, again, the clock was ticking.

So, once again, I prayed as I drove from our house to the storage lot to do some simple refurbishing work on the bus. "OK, Lord. You know I have no clue where to get this stuff done to the bus. And this trip is really important to Lana. I really need your help."

Just a couple hundred yards before the entrance to the storage lot, I noticed a sign above a building just off the road. I had passed this way countless times before and never even noticed the building or the sign. The sign indicated that it was a truck garage. The lot in front of the build was littered with big rig tractors and trailers of all sorts in some state of brokenness or repair. So, into the parking lot I went.

Oh, sure. Some well-dressed old guy driving a four door sedan is really going to command respect around a bunch of diesel mechanics. I was sure that I would either get laughed out of the building or thrown out. But, in I went anyway. There was a lady behind a counter in the office. I explained that I needed to know if they could do an oil change in my bus. She said that I needed to talk to the head mechanic. So, out into the garage I went.

Well, it took a couple of minutes to find someone who wasn't stuffed under a truck head-first to talk with. I told the first upright guy I found that I was looking for the head mechanic. He pointed me to specific pair of feet sticking out from under another truck. So, I went over and waited until I had more than feet to talk to. I explained to him that I had just bought a bus and the main engine and generator both needed an oil change. He explained that the garage had been built to maintain the fleet of trucks for its owner. But, (*Here comes the grace. Can you feel it?*), they do perform some commercial work. He would be glad to get me worked in.

Wow! A well-equipped, experienced diesel garage less than a quarter of a mile from where we had our bus stored that was able and willing to work on our bus. Once again it seemed that fate was smiling on us. Well, we all know it was way more than fate.

PEELING BACK THE YEARS

Our bus had been beautifully decorated by the builder's wife. She did a great job of selecting colors and materials that would look great and stand the test of time. One of the two couches in the lounge area was light gray leather. I am sure that it had once looked great. But now, while the leather was physically in good shape, its appearance left a lot to be desired. Let me put it this way: it reminded me of one of the old couches I used to see in airplane hangars back in my flying days. You know the kind. It was once the pride of the house, but started to look pretty bad and had been relegated to the basement for the kids to play on. Eventually, it looked too bad for even the basement, so it got put in a garage sale, and ended up in some guy's hangar, where greasy pants regularly collapsed on it for a brief respite before getting back to working on the airplane engine. Yeah. That couch.

So, anyway it needed something done to it. I had no idea whether or not leather like this was cleanable, or if we would need to replace the couch altogether. And, if it had to be replaced, I had no clue as to what type of couch we would need to buy for a bus, where we would be able to buy one, or if we could even physically get the old one out and the new one in. Plus, our planned departure date was closing in. Yep. That old clock was ticking again.

I happened upon the name of a local company that supposedly did leather repairs. I don't even recall how I came by it. I didn't know if they could clean our couch, or not. But, as Lana has told me on many occasions, "You're already at NO. You've got nothing to lose by asking." So, I called them.

A couple of days later I met a young man from the leather company at the bus. He was quite optimistic as to its potential, and got right to work. A couple of hours later, I stood in front of what could have passed for a brand new light gray leather couch. It was beautiful. And the cost was very modest. Again, I was shocked that fate had once again smiled on us. Yeah. Right.

Then, there was the furnace. On the trip home from Virginia with the bus, it got cool during our night in the Wal-Mart parking lot. So, I fired up the two gas furnaces in the bus. They both blew air, but only the front unit heated, which didn't do us much good in the rear bedroom. I didn't worry too much about it at the time. But, since we were headed into mountainous country in a few weeks, I thought we might need it. But, again I had no idea who might work on an old RV gas furnace. There were several RV dealers around town, but they mostly had travel trailers and fifth-wheels and very small shops. I seriously doubted that they would entertain working on an RV they had not sold, much less an old converted bus.

I recalled an RV dealer that Lana and I had visited one afternoon just looking at some small motorhomes as we were entertaining the idea or maybe buying something. They also had a large truck and farm implement dealership associated with their RV business, and a very large shop. So, I called. The lady I spoke with was most accommodating and scheduled a service appointment for us.

When we took our bus to their shop, I met one of the owners, who happened to manage the shop part of the business. He was quite taken with our old bus. He even related to me that he had always wanted to convert a bus like this. We had a friend!

When they got into the furnace, they found the problem, which was not too difficult to fix. But, they had to completely disassemble the furnace to do so, which would mean breaking open a sealed assembly. This meant that a key gasket would need to be replaced. But, the trouble was that the furnace was old and replacement gaskets were no longer available. Once again, it seems as though we were all dressed up with nowhere to go, as they say.

The service manager asked what I wanted to do. I told him that the furnace didn't do us any good as it was, so go ahead and see if they could fix it somehow.

Well, as you might suspect, when he called back a couple of days later, he said that the furnace was all fixed and good to go. It seems that when they disassembled the furnace the old gasket did not get destroyed as he thought it would. It wasn't even damaged. They were able to reuse it.

Yes sir. Things were really going our way. What luck! (*Wink, wink*)

A LOOSE SCREW

I am sure that we would all agree that steering in a vehicle of any type and size is important, be it car, bicycle, truck, or a bus. It gets increasingly important as the vehicle's speed and weight increases and the driver's experience decreases.

So, let's go back in time to the day we test drove our bus. I recall thinking that the steering had a lot of play, and mentioned it to the previous owner. He assured me that all was in order. That was just how a bus felt. What did I know? That was the only bus I had ever driven. So, that was all that was said about that.

As we started toward home with our new purchase that spring evening, I was pretty well occupied just trying to wrap my head around operating something as big as a bus. But I did notice that as we got up to highway speeds, I was having a difficult time keeping the bus in the lane. It kept wanting to drift to the right and then back to the left with no warning. I wrote it off to my inexperience, and just resolved to myself that I would just have to fight it until I got used to it.

Do you recall when you first started driving, and the first time you passed another car? Remember the feeling that your life and that of the other driver and any passengers involved all depended upon your driving skill and you not screwing up? Well, multiply that by about 40,000 pounds. Every time another vehicle went past us, my life flashed before my eyes. I just knew that one of those unpredictable lane drifts would come just at the wrong time and end everyone's trip real quick. But, I just kept snapping that old bus back into our lane, and tried to look like I knew what I was doing. That was a long 600 miles, let me tell you! But we made it safely.

Fast forward to when the bus was getting its first oil change with my "just down the road" mechanic. He was a very down to earth, old country mechanic. He got the oil and the filters all changed. But, when I dropped the bus off at his garage, I mentioned the steering and asked him to take a quick look if he had time. When I went to pick-up the bus, I asked him if he had the chance to look at the steering. He replied with a calm tone that he did, and that the steering bear box was loose. This is the part that connects the actual steering column to the front wheels. A pretty key part. Anyway, as we chatted he casually mentioned that of the four bolts that held that steering box to the bus, two were loose and two were gone!

Gone? As in "not there"? My heart was in my throat. I had just driven 600 miles in that bus with my bride in the bus with me, with the steering in that condition. Only two loose bolts stood between us and eternity for 600 miles!

After I dropped the bus off in the storage lot, I headed back home. It was as I drove home that it began to dawn on me that all of our good fortune and luck with the bus was way more than that. I had a very strong and clear sense that God's hand was on our bus and on this entire endeavor. I couldn't put many of the other pieces together in my mind, but I was certain that his hand had been on all of these events. But on a bus? Why would he possibly choose to help with the details of owning an old bus?

This awareness was to resurface on many occasions.

BLACK FRIDAY

Well, the date for our departure on our long inaugural trip in the bus was at hand. We planned to leave on Saturday headed for the Black Hills of South Dakota and many points in between. We were both looking forward to really using our bus, but Lana seemed especially excited about the trip. So, late Friday afternoon I went to the storage lot to check the bus over and make sure that it was ready to hit the road the next day.

Being a meticulous person, I had a list of stuff that I wanted to check. You know. Stuff like engine oil and coolant levels, air pressure in all eight of the tires, and the generator. The generator was important because it was summer, and anyone who has ever spent any time in northwest Ohio in the summer knows that it can be humid and most uncomfortable. So, air conditioning as we drove was highly desirable. And, the bus's three roof-top air conditioners require the generator to provide adequate electrical power. So, a thorough check out of the generator was also on my list.

I checked everything I knew to check, but noticed that I could not see the fan belt that is used to drive a cooling fan for the generator. I knew that I should look into this even though I was not familiar at all with the generator. So, I got a flashlight and dug into the generator bay as far as I could. I finally noticed that the pulley on the electric motor that runs the fan was missing. How could an entire three inch pulley disappear from a sealed bay? I looked around using the flashlight as well as I could, but no pulley in sight.

What would I do now? The pulley was missing-in-action, we were planning to leave the next day, and we needed the generator in order to make the trip. I sank into a brief bit of panic. I had never worked on a generator before. Then, it hit me. My diesel mechanic was just down the street. I would get him or one of the other mechanics to come take a look. I bet they could figure it out and get it fixed. But, then I noticed that it was after 5:00pm on a Friday afternoon. In the unlikely event any of the mechanics were around, I was certain that they would have no interest in helping me with a generator fan problem that close to "Miller time".

So, I talked it over with God, as had become my habit. Not really asking for his intervention or help, but admitting that it was out of my hands. If the generator was to be fixed and we were to be able to leave the following day on our trip, it would be up to God. I turned it over to him.

Then, I thought, let me shove an arm into this concentration of diesel engine and high voltage electrical components to see if I could feel something that might be helpful. What choice did I really have? If I couldn't see it, maybe, just maybe I could feel it. Although I wasn't quite sure what I would do if I happened to find it, I had to do something. I certainly wasn't excited about this idea, but it was all I had. So, kneeling on the ground, into the generator bay I went – up to my shoulder. Feeling around for the pulley. It wasn't in the back. Maybe up by the electric fan motor. Nope. Perhaps somewhere around the fan itself. Nada. OK. All that was left was the very front of the generator bay, up by the outer wall. Wait. What is that I feel? It is metal. But so is almost everything else in that bay. I could tell that what I was feeling was round. Maybe, just maybe …

I managed to get a very tenuous grip on it with two fingers and eased it back to where I could grab it. It was the missing pulley. Hallelujah!

But that was only a small part of the problem. Now, I had to figure out how this contraption worked and get it fixed. I knew that the pulley had to go onto the electric motor shaft. A quick examination of the pulley revealed that it was not a keyed pulley, so how did it fasten onto the motor shaft. Ah-ha! There was a hole for a set screw in the pulley. That must simply tighten onto the motor shaft. But I did not see a set screw, which is a very small screw. Close but no cigar.

I noticed that the set screw hole had a bunch of grease and debris in it. So, I cleaned some of this gunk out, and there was the set screw. It was right where it needed to be and seemingly intact. But it would require a somewhat uncommon tool to tighten it. Bummer.

But, just the prior week I had purchased a collection of tools to keep on the bus. I had simply guessed at generic tools that I thought might come in handy. Of course, not being familiar with the bus or what tools might be needed, it was truly a wild guess. I poked through the bus's tool box, and found a bunch of varied fastener drivers that were part of a small ratchet and socket set. And, sure enough one of them was exactly the right type and size that I needed for the set screw.

So, a few more minutes with my arm into the generator bay, I figured out how everything fit together. Then, with a bit more effort I had it back together, tested, and ready for action.

I had repaired a critical component on the bus we had owned for about 60 days, blindly finding the missing part, using tools that I had no knowledge I might need but just happened to have purchased. I was feeling pretty proud. Then it hit me. I had not really made that repair. All I did was to shove my arm into the bay and hold the tool. The true Master Mechanic had done the real work.

Over the days and weeks that followed I began to ask myself if, perhaps God really had a hand in all of these events. If so, why would he have an interest in us having and being able to travel in this old bus?

My apologies for the flood of technical descriptions related to the generator repair. I am an engineer and it is to be expected, I guess. But, I saw God's hand in every step and detail of this event. But I have come to know – really know – that no detail is too small for our awesome God. Even the tiniest set screw in a pulley is important to him, if it is important to us. Especially if it is to be used to help one of his children in trouble.

MAIDEN VOYAGE

Being much older and wiser (*Well, OK. Maybe just older.*), I look back now and wonder at why in the world would we plan to take this bus, about which we knew very little, and with which I had virtually zero experience on a 2,500 mile trip through the vast farmland of Iowa and South Dakota, back along the Canadian border and down through Michigan? Were we nuts? Perhaps. But off we went anyway, driving on 2 lane back roads, and hundreds upon hundreds of miles of freeway. After all. What could go wrong?

Throughout this green-horn trip, we saw a great deal of our beautiful country that neither of us had ever seen. We greatly enjoyed each other's company – just spending time together. We met other wonderful people. We made many, many happy memories. In short – it was a great trip with no real rough spots.

As I reflected on our maiden voyage with our old bus, I could not help but feel, once again, that God's hand had been on every detail of this trip. With all that could have gone wrong (*and probably should have gone wrong*), we arrived back home safe and sound with many great stories to share and many great memories to cherish, and not a thread of connection to the past.

I began to see that this might well be the catalyst that would help Lana (*and me*) to move ahead.

MR. BUS, MEET MR. TREE

Well, there was one small hiccup on our maiden voyage. Our last stop was in the upper-peninsula of Michigan, on the shores of Lake Huron. We spent several days there enjoying the serenity of the beautiful forest and the great weather. We even spent a day on Mackinac Island (*No, not in the bus*), and yes – the fudge is out of this world!

Finally the day came when we were to head home. It had been a great trip. So, we got all packed up, fired up the old bus and pulled out.

One thing I have learned through our bus experiences is that many places – even RV parks and campgrounds – are not designed for or well suited to 40 foot buses.

So, we eased along through the campground, headed for the office and the main gate. There was a pretty sharp turn by the office, then it was clear sailing. I had made the turn (*in the opposite direction*) when we checked in, so I was not concerned. "What could go wrong?"

Well, my focus was more on the road than on the 40 feet of bus following me. I edged over to the right to make sure that I would be able to stay on the road throughout the left turn. We eased along. Then, "Bang!"

"Bang?" Our bus wasn't supposed to go "Bang". So, I stopped and got out looking for the source of the big bang (*no pun intended*). Then I noticed the rear support for our 21 foot long side awning dangling from the top, torn loose from its bottom attachment. I was no awning expert, but I was pretty sure that awning supports aren't supposed to dangle.

When I put all of the pieces of the puzzle together, I realized that when I had eased to the right for the turn, I had gotten close – WAY too close – to a tree that was right at the edge of the roadway. The tree had caught the awning support and torn it away from the bus, destroying its bottom support.

Well, nuts. I certainly did not have any spare awning parts with me. We had a 350 mile drive ahead of us, and I certainly couldn't just let the support dangle down the freeway. Plus, this bottom support played a key role in keeping the awning attached to the bus. Unless it was properly secured, I feared that the awning would be torn off of the bus entirely as we drove down the highway.

Time out. Time to take a short trip down another bunny trail. I have never been known as a patient guy, especially when I am responsible for something or someone. I spent my working life being responsible for delivering a service to over one hundred thousand people, and really being under the gun when they experienced a disruption to get it resolved "yesterday". So, being responsible for a bus full of equipment and systems and with my bride onboard, and having something go wrong while we were hundreds of miles from home was a familiar but unpleasant experience. I had to do something and do it now!

OK. Back to our regularly scheduled program.

As I pondered (*a better word would be worried*) about what I was going to do to get this fixed and us on the road home, it occurred to me that I had a section of rope in the cargo bay. Not too sure why I had put it there in the first place. We didn't need to tie anything down while we drove, nor when we setup camp. I had not needed it to this point. But, yet there it was. So, I dug around in the cargo bay, pulled it out, and did a tying job on that awning support that would have made Rube Goldberg proud. It seemed secure enough. But, I knew that the rigors of freeway driving would tell us for sure if it would hold.

Some six hours later we pulled up in front of our house. As I inspected my little knitting job with the rope, I found that it was still tight and secure. It had held just fine.

Once again, God had shown his grace to an impatient old man through his experiences with an old bus in the fact that the awning support had been the only damage, and that fairly minor, in the fact that there just "happened" to be a section of rope onboard, and, in the fact that we made it home safe and sound with no additional damage.

As a footnote: the company that manufactured the awning that had been damaged was no longer in business, so parts were not readily available. I just happened to find (*wink, wink*) a guy in the state of Oregon who had purchased all of the old company's parts. He just happened to have (*wink, wink*) the part that I needed to repair our awning costing us only about $30. Yes sir. "If grace is an ocean, we're all sinking".

BABY, IT'S COLD OUTSIDE

What a great maiden voyage. We had travelled some 2,500 miles in the bus and had a great time. But, summer was done and fall was upon us. In northern Ohio, fall is just a 2 minute warning for winter. Winters here can be long, very cold and very snowy. So, we thought it best if we could store the bus inside for the winter, to keep it out of the extreme weather. How hard can it be to find inside storage for a bus? There have to be hundreds and hundreds of other RV-ers in this area who store their RVs inside. So, all we have to do is to find one of these places.

As you might have guessed, that was easier said than done. I talked to some people who knew some other people who knew a guy whose cousin used to work for a lady whose father used to have an RV stored inside a building somewhere. Yeah, that was how my search went. I was getting nowhere fast and the weather was getting cooler every day.

Then, I stumbled upon a guy who was managing a very large building for its out-of-town owners. The building had been a large automotive manufacturing plant that had shut down, and they were renting heated storage space to RV owners until they could find a permanent tenant or a new owner. So, I called this guy and asked about it. It sounded great. A little pricey, but heated and fairly close to us. I asked him to send me the storage agreement so I could look it over, really just as a formality. I was sure that it would be OK.

A fellow I used to work for told me many times that "the devil is in the details" and that sure turned out to be the case with this deal. The storage agreement required that I hand over the keys to our bus to the people running the storage operation. It stated that they could cancel the agreement with 30 days' notice – even in the dead of winter. But, the real clincher was that they were not responsible for anything. Oh sure. I'll give you the keys to our beautiful bus so you can drive it out and use it for a demolition derby, target practice or as a project for a body shop school and I'll pay for whatever repairs might be required when I pick it up, IF it's still there. As was frequently heard on a popular TV show in the 1990's; "I don't think so, Tim."

It was true that winter was closing in fast, and we needed indoor heated storage for the bus, but it didn't take me long to file that agreement in the proverbial round filing cabinet and move on.

By this time we had already had several nights with the temperature well below freezing and a few light snows. Yep. I could definitely hear old man winter's footsteps. Then I just happened to see a post on an online classified ad website that a guy had a big barn that he was wanting to rent space in. So, I called him up. It turned out that this option would work great with no ornery agreement terms to get in the way. But, it was not heated.

Who was I to look askance at a solution to our problem? So, into the barn we went. As it turns out, we were his only tenant that winter. The barn was big, easy to get to, and the owner was most accommodating.

Within a couple of weeks after we put the bus to bed in the barn, the coldest and snowiest winter we have experienced in the 30+ years we have lived in northern Ohio hit us full force. I am confident that our bus would not have fared well out in the elements. It was lucky (*wink, wink*) that we found inside storage when we did.

DOWN TO THE RIVER TO PRAY

After the coldest and harshest winter in memory, we decided that we would spend some time in warmer climes and visit family in Arkansas. So, as summer approached, we made plans to spend a couple of weeks camped with family in the Ozarks. The Bull Shoals–White River State Park is truly one of the most beautiful park settings we have seen. It set along the shores of the White River, just below the Bull Shoals dam. The cold water of the river and beautiful scenery make a stay in this park a real vacation. Plus, the trout fishing there is world famous.

For you history buffs, the White River – yes, this White River – came to prominence in the early years of the Clinton administration. This was the heart of a widely publicized real estate scandal.

So, we camped along the beautiful White River, enjoying the scenery, the weather, and the company of family. But, all good things must come to an end and the day of our departure drew near. So, the evening before we were planning to pull out, I donned my rain gear (*Yeah. That was the only time it rained the entire time we were there.*) and started checking the bus over in preparation for the return trip. Everything looked fine. Last thing I checked was the generator, which as was mentioned earlier is a necessity for summer travel for the roof top air conditioning units as we drove. Oil was fine. Coolant was fine. The cooling fan . . . Where is the fan belt? No fan belt (*You guessed it. This was the same fan belt that had plagued us before our maiden trip.*). So, onto my knees I went (*Not to pray . . . yet. Just to get my hands into the generator bay.*).

After a good bit of fumbling and feeling around, I discovered the root of our problem: the steel bracket that holds the electric fan motor had broken. Not just a crack or a small "boo-boo", but it was broken in half. So, there I was, kneeling in the rain and mud, with my arms into the generator bay up to my shoulders, with a broken bus and no way to fix it.

God doesn't cause bad things to happen to us. We live in a broken world, and sometimes stuff just happens. But, I do believe that God will use these bad things to help us to grow if we will let him.

As long as I was already down on my knees, I prayed; really, I whined. I explained what God already knew; that the bus was broken and I had no clue what to do about it. I did not have the tools or materials to fix it. If we were to leave the next morning, it would be up to him.

In my own way, I had turned it over to God; left this problem at the foot of the Cross. It was out of my hands. I was no longer responsible for the outcome. I believe to this day that was exactly what God wanted me to do – wants us all to do – come to him with our problems and leave them at the foot of the Cross.

Through this problem (*and many more to follow*), God began teaching me patience. When I am in the middle of a situation that I don't have an immediate resolution for, just sit back and take a breath. Most things are not as urgent as I tend to make them out to be (*But, after all, I was conditioned to do just that in my working life.*). A resolution will come, always in God's time and almost universally NOT in my time.

So, back to the broken generator.

I walked down to where my bride and some of her family were playing cards and explained the problem. My brother-in-law inquired as to the nature of the problem. I laid the details out for him. I just happened to have removed the broken part just to show Lana, so I handed that to my brother-in-law as if to say, "See. I told you it was broken."

He knew a fellow that was a skilled welder and fabricator. He called him at home and explained the problem. He said that he would be glad to take a look first thing in the morning, and agreed to meet my brother-in-law at his shop at 7:00am.

At least there was a light at the end of the tunnel. Only time would tell if it was the dawn or a train.

Sure enough, about 8:30 the next morning up drives my brother-in-law with the repaired part in hand. I was speechless. Actually, I was embarrassed that I did not realize that God was bigger than a broken metal bracket. How could I have doubted or even been concerned that it would not work out OK?

Once again, God had showered us with his grace, this time through a broken metal bracket, a caring brother-in-law, and a welder I will probably never meet.

WHAT'S THAT SMELL?

The second summer or our bus owning adventure, we decided to take a trip down the east coast visiting many of the Civil War battlefields, swinging by to visit our bus's builder and his wife, and then back home. For me, this was one of the most meaningful and moving trips I have ever taken. We were both deeply moved as we stood in the places where thousands upon thousands of young men gave their lives for what they believed. I would make this trip again in a New York minute!

Anyway, we had been on the road for a couple of weeks, and were headed home. It was a drizzly, muggy day, so I was running the dash air conditioning, but not the roof top units. About an hour from home, Lana went to the galley, and came right back and asked me, "What's that smell?" I didn't smell anything. She insisted saying that it smelled like burning rubber. This did not sound like good news.

So, at the next exit, we pulled off and parked in a carry-out parking lot. I jumped out, and trotted the rear of the bus, and saw smoke coming out of the engine compartment. Since our bus did not have the smoke screen option installed, I was pretty sure that something was not right. I yelled at my co-pilot to get out of the bus just in case, which she promptly did. When I swung the door to the engine compartment open, I saw the problem. The compressor for the dash air conditioning unit I had been running all day had seized up, and the rubber belts that provided its power from the engine were simply sliding over the compressor's motionless pulley at very high speed, and had been doing so for a while, making the pulley very hot. Since we had stopped, the belts that were now motionless on the pulley got so hot they had melted and were bubbling, close to actually burning.

So, here we were, an hour from home and near the end of the working day (*about 5:00pm*). The melted belts also provided power for other crucial engine components, so we weren't going anywhere. The bus was disabled. We were in a strange town where I knew no one.

Once again, the bus for which I was responsible was on the fritz. I was unable to get my wife home, and had absolutely no clue what to do.

However, we had just recently contracted with a new road-side service company. Our experience with the old one is worth a book all by itself. Let's just say we had found them to be unsatisfactory. Not really expecting much after our experiences with the prior company, I gave our new company a call. After answering a bunch of questions I was finally informed that a service technician would be dispatched and should arrive within two hours. Two hours? What were we supposed to do for two hours in the parking lot of a carry-out?

Once again, it was beyond my control. There was absolutely nothing more I could do about. Do you recall that I mentioned earlier that God was teaching me patience through our experiences in the bus? Well, this must have been a graduate level course, and I don't think my grade was very good. After pacing around for what seemed like forever, I eventually went into the carry out and explained our dilemma to the guy behind the counter, telling him that I was not sure how long we would be there. He said OK, but really didn't seem to care much either way.

Well, after what seemed like hours (*actually, only about 40 minutes*), a service truck pulled up. The technician said that he had only been a few minutes away, and came over as soon as he finished the job he had been working on. After some discussion and tinkering, we agreed that we would abandon the dash air conditioner and belt around the problematic compressor just to get the bus on the road again. He took a couple of measurements and drove off in search of the belts we needed.

Not more than 30 minutes later he returned. And in less than another 30 minutes he had completed the repair. Now, the bill. The inevitable bill. But, when he handed it to me, I was shocked. It was for about $30. It seems that our road side assistance agreement provided for two hours of a mechanic's time for each event/problem as part of the annual fee. Since he did not have to drive but a few minutes to our bus, he did not go beyond the two hours. All we had to pay for was the two new belts.

So, about two hours and 30 bucks later, we were back on our way. Once again God had shown us his love and grace, and had shown me my lack of patience (*again*). The problem could have been very serious. We could have lost the bus to a fire. We could have broken down in the middle of nowhere. The road side repair could have been WAY expensive. But, none of these things came to pass.

I was just beginning to understand just how extreme God's love for us is. But, why us? Why this old bus?

TRANNY FLU

When we purchased the bus, the builder told us that the transmission was a used heavy truck transmission that he had purchased and installed along with a newly rebuilt engine. It worked OK, but even though it was an automatic transmission, you had to shift it manually. We wisely set as a condition of our purchase that the transmission had to shift automatically as designed. This repair was made before we drove it home, and worked satisfactorily for a couple of years and thousands of miles.

The diesel garage that we had used down the street from our storage lot had worked fine for us so far. But, as time wore on, the mechanics there became more and more consumed with the repair of their own fleet of trucks, and had less and less time to do commercial work (*work on our bus*). We would have to wait sometimes for weeks before the smallest things would be tended to. Even though I understood and was completely sympathetic, we needed to find a more available shop.

I inquired of people I knew that had RVs and they all used local RV dealers (*I was not surprised to find no one else who had a converted coach like ours*). I could have tried that route, I guess, but our bus is more like a big truck than a motorhome. So, I asked a friend who had driven over-the-road in big rigs for years and was now teaching at a local truck driving school. He pointed me to any one of several shops at major freeway intersection just on the other side of town. He was confident that any of the shops there would be very good. So, after a bit of additional research on my part, I discovered that one of those shops was factory certified to perform work on both our particular engine and transmission. So, we decided to give them a try.

Our initial trip to the new mechanic shop was for a couple of simple tasks and an oil change. They did a great job, even taking care of a couple of other minor things that needed attention at no additional cost. OK. So, we had found a new garage.

One spring, I was working to get the bus ready for our summer travels, and wanted to have our new garage check the bus over and take care of a few relatively minor mechanical issues. I also asked them to check the transmission. Over time it had reached a point where, at a relatively low speed it would flutter back and forth between 2nd and 3rd gear, usually in the middle of an intersection or as we started off up an incline. It had concerned me on a couple of occasions, so I felt it needed to be resolved once and for all.

A few days later I had a call from the service manager at the shop. He said that a major component in the transmission was in very bad shape and could fail at any time, rendering the bus un-drivable and leaving us stranded. I double checked with a friend who had worked on this type of transmission and he confirmed that it was not a good situation, and really should be fixed.

We opted to simply replace the transmission with a newly re-manufactured one; a pricey option, but the safest for my precious cargo. Our shop did a great job of swapping out the transmission. But along the way, the mechanic realized that the way the builder had setup the accelerator pedal, the transmission would never work as it should. But, since the bus was so old, a replacement for what we needed was unavailable. Undaunted, the service manager and their chief mechanic set to work designing and building a custom accelerator module. It worked great.

Once again, God had shown us his grace by guiding us to a shop that had the expertise, capacity and compassion to fix this major issue and the creativity to keep a 50 year old bus on the road. They had almost certainly prevented us from being stranded along the road.

By the way, the new transmission and accelerator work great, and the old bus shifts as smooth as a Cadillac – a VERY big Cadillac.

OH, PUDDLE!

After we had owned the bus for a few years, we had several trips planned in the bus over the upcoming summer. So, we thought it would be wise to take a late spring shake-down trip. So, we headed to one of Ohio's beautiful state parks on the shores of Lake Erie. Since we planned to remain in the park, and only for a couple of days, we did not bring our scooter (*We have a 35 year old scooter that we sometimes bring with us on a ramp behind the bus. This gives us a way to make milk and bread runs if we need to.*). This time we only brought our bicycles so we could take leisurely rides around the park.

We arrived at the park in the late afternoon, checked in, and found our spot. Lana started setting everything up inside, while I got to work hooking us up to electricity, water, etc. When I got all finished, I noticed a small puddle of water under the bus at a spot where there should be no water. But, with this being our first time out that year, I just figured it was a little water that had spilled while I was filling the fresh water tank. But, several minutes later, I noticed the small puddle had grown into a medium-sized puddle. Something was not as it should be. After a brief investigation, I determined that the water was coming from the hot water heater. Not good.

"To the toolbox, BusMan!" OK. So, maybe that's a bit over dramatic. I grabbed a handful of tools and began tearing into the hot water heater. I discovered that the main drain valve in the tank was leaking: it would not close all the way. It was probably the original valve and had worked fine for many years. But, now, in the middle of a state park, 20 miles from anywhere, with no way to travel other than in the bus itself, and with no clue where I might happen to find a valve for a 20 year old RV hot water heater, it decided to stop working.

I didn't know if the part I needed would be unique to an RV water heater, or if it might be a more generic plumbing part. But I had to do something. Frustrated, and having no other options, I began looking online for an RV shop or plumbing shop close-by. All I was able to find was a big-box home improvement store about 20 miles away. So, having no real option, we packed everything up, unhooked the bus from the park facilities, and off we went in search of the part we needed, having no real chance of finding it, especially late on a Friday afternoon.

If we were unable to find the part we needed, our only option was to return home that night and forget all about the trip. Needless to say, my driving included a continuous silent prayer. I found the home improvement store, went in and asked where the plumbing parts were. After a brief search I found where the lead-free brass valves were shelved. There was the box bearing the label of exactly the valve I needed. Awesome! But, the box was empty.

My heart sank once again. Close but no cigar. Without really even thinking about it, I began rummaging through the adjacent boxes, not really sure what I expected to find. And there, mixed in with other valves of different sizes in another box was a valve with a label different from the others in that box. I grabbed it and read the specs on its label. It was exactly the part that I needed! There in the middle of the plumbing isle in a big-box home improvement store, God had shown me yet again that no detail of my life is too small for him: that he is bigger than a leaky valve.

About $20 later, I returned to the bus part in hand. Before I even started the bus, I grabbed the necessary tools and put the new valve in place in the parking lot. It was a perfect fit. I should have never doubted.

TRANNY FLU RELAPSE

That summer included several trips in the bus. But, the big trip for the summer was a trip to the Ozarks to see family. We had made this trip several times before, but this summer it would be a special trip: our youngest son and his bride, our two grandchildren, and our daughter-in-law's brother would be making the trip with us. We had never taken a trip with anyone else in the bus with us. This was going to be great!

The trip is normally a 13 to 14 hour drive, making for a long day's drive, which we had made many times before. But, this time we planned to spread the trip over two days. We did not plan to leave until about noon, which would mean that, if we drove straight through we would arrive in the middle of the night. Also, the bus does not provide comfortable sleeping accommodations for that many people. So, we would drive about halfway, and spend the night in a hotel.

We arrived at our stopping point around suppertime. I was strongly urged by my passengers that we should get something to eat before checking into the hotel, especially since we had no other means of transportation other than the bus. Food to teenagers means pizza. So, we found a pizza place with a big shopping center parking lot next door (*which was required to park a 40 foot bus*).

I shut the bus down as my son and grandson went for pizza. Some 15 to 20 minutes later, here they came, pizza boxes in hand. Now, to the hotel and a bit of supper and relaxing. So, I hit the starter on the bus. Nothing. I tried again. Not a sound. I checked everything I could think of: gear selector in neutral, ignition on. No change. Here we were, seven people stranded in the parking lot of a shopping center a long way from home and from anyone who might be able to help us. I was responsible for these people, and was helpless.

Frustration and prayer don't usually make good bedfellows, but they both accompanied me that evening. I had no idea what to do, but I knew that I needed to do something. So, instinctively a silent prayer was said as my son and I popped open the engine hatch not knowing what to expect, or having any idea what we would do if we found something. We checked what we knew to check, and not surprisingly found nothing.

All I had left was to call the roadside assistance company that we contracted with. They had been great for us, but it can take a while to actually get someone onsite. So, I called them and explained our dilemma. I was told that a qualified diesel technician would call me back within an hour or two. An "hour or two?" Perfect. Here I was responsible for 6 of the people dearest to me and all I could do was to wait for a phone call in a strange parking lot.

My family was great about the whole thing. They opened up the pizza and made the best of it. All I could do was to worry and stew.

About an hour later there was still no call from our roadside assistance technician. Just out of habit and frustration, I tried to start the bus again, and it fired right up! I didn't spend any time trying to figure out what happened or why: I just headed for the hotel. At least we would have a safe place to sleep.

Early the next morning I called the mechanic shop at home that worked on our bus. I explained the problem to the service manager. We discussed the possible causes, but he was certain that the problem was caused by a little switch in the transmission that determined if the gear selector was in neutral making it safe to start. He felt it was sensitive to heat, explaining why the bus started after cooling off for a while. We decided that it was safe to continue on our trip, but we should make sure that whenever we shut the bus down, that we are where we wanted to be for a while. He even explained an emergency wire-around just in case I might need it.

Here again, while I was worrying about my responsibility for taking care of my family, those people who mean the most to me, God was taking care of us all; I was just too consumed with worry and frustration to recognize it.

CHAPTER 5

HALFTIME UPDATE

Yes sir. This whole "bus" thing had been quite a ride. First, we would have never in our wildest dreams thought that we would ever own a bus, not to mention a 50 year-old bus. I would have never imagined that I would have been able to restore and maintain a classic bus that had been converted into a motorhome. Neither my bride nor I would have ever thought that we would be travelling the country in a self-contained ultimate hippie bus, doing things we had only heard of and never even spoken of doing. But, here we were, doing all of these things and having little to do with the outcome ourselves.

As I reflected on the whole experience so far and on all of the challenges and problems that I had encountered, it began to sink in just how God's hand had been on this whole thing. The chance repairs, the avoided accidents, things that were so far beyond my abilities as to be laughable: I could now clearly see God's hand in our old bus.

More importantly, I could clearly see God's hand in working to allow Lana to do something that she enjoyed – really enjoyed, which had no connection at all to our daughter. God had used this old bus to help Lana begin to heal and to live again. There were no lightning bolts, no parted sea, no water surging from a rock – but a miracle nonetheless. He had used an old bus and an incompetent husband to heal his precious child. Love beyond compare. Grace without bounds.

I was – and remain – humbled that the Creator of the universe had seen fit to intervene in the lives of two of his children, and use the uncommon, the unusual, the unconventional to help restore them and to demonstrate to them just how precious they are to him, and that there is nothing he won't do for them.

So, he had worked his miracle and set us both on the road to life again. What a ride it had been. But, as a friend of mine has told me many times, "the best is yet to come".

CHAPTER 6

Snowbirds

Most people dream of retiring, of not having to work every day and being able to do whatever we want to do, not what someone tells us to do. Lana and I have long discussed our hopeful retirement and what we would like to do. She has never liked the cold weather, and so, naturally we live in northern Ohio. During our earlier retirement discussions she had mentioned wanting move to somewhere warm when we retired. Since this was not my idea of a good time we had tabled the whole discussion, knowing that we would resume the whole discussion someday.

Before I retired, grandchildren entered our lives, which changed our whole retirement discussion. Living close to grandchildren, as you might suspect, is very high on the list for both of us. Since they only live a couple of miles away and are a routine and very important part of our lives, moving to a warmer climate and away from them was no longer an option. As the bus entered our lives, Lana's desire for a warmer climate morphed into our retirement conversation of years earlier where we would spend the cold winter months in a warmer place without actually moving. Now this seemed to be the ideal solution, just as we had tentatively agreed years earlier. All we had to do was to find a place to park, drive there and enjoy the warm weather. Simple, right?

HELLO, DOLLY

All of the trips we had taken so far in the bus were of fairly short duration: two to three weeks at best. We could plan on swinging by a grocery store in the bus as we moved from one place to another to pick-up whatever supplies we might need. Or, when we would stay in one place a bit longer, I could always jump on the scooter and make a run to the grocery store or the laundromat. Now we were talking about spending three or four months in the bus. We would frequently need to go to the grocery store, to church, to other places. Plus, we would to go places together. Our bicycles would not work, nor would the scooter (*even if Lana would dare get on it with me*). The solution was obvious: we would need a car with us over the winter.

We looked at possibly renting a car at our winter destination, but either no one seemed to be willing to do this or it was prohibitively expensive. Option B was to tow one of our cars. But, none of our vehicles is towable with all four wheels on the road. Plus, we did not have a tow hitch.

So, on to option C: buy a tow dolly. This would allow us to tow one of our vehicles with the front wheels off the road. Perfect. The only vehicle we have that is a front wheel drive was Lana's Honda Civic. So, that was the plan. But which tow dolly to get?

I researched all of the options, reading more reviews from fellow RV-ers than I could recount. One of the problems that surfaced quickly was storage: where would we store this thing when we were at home? We live in a small residential neighborhood, where we are not permitted to store anything outside. Our garage is not large enough to accommodate a traditional tow dolly along with our vehicles. Since we store the bus in an outdoor lot during the warm months, we could always get another storage spot there. But that would mean that it would be exposed to the weather. Not a good idea. We finally found a dolly that was able to be stored standing upright. Perfect. That would fit into our garage along with all of our vehicles and other garage stuff. Problem solved.

After a couple of conversations with the manufacturer to make sure that it would work with our Honda Civic I placed the order for the tow dolly. When it arrived, I got it put together, carefully measuring the placement of the ramps to line up with the wheels on the Civic. The only thing remaining was to hook the dolly up to the bus, load the Civic and take a quick test drive around town just to make sure that we had everything we needed and knew how it all fit together.

So, one bright fall day I brought the bus home and hooked up the tow dolly. It took a while, but I finally managed to get the dolly secured and all of the lights working as they should. Lana came out to drive the Civic onto the dolly as I watched and guided her. Slowly and carefully she drove onto the ramps, eased up the ramp inch-by-inch. Finally at the top, just before easing the tires into their cradle I saw that it was not going to fit onto the dolly. The car was too low, making the bottom of the car's engine hit the tow dolly's primary support. Bummer.

We would not be able to make a long-term trip without a car, meaning that the planned winter trip was out of the question. We had purchased the only tow dolly that we could effectively use, but it would not work for the only car we owned that could tow. And we had hoped to depart within the next 30 days.

A quick call to the manufacturer yielded no help. They told me that they had many customers who successfully towed a Honda Civic with their dolly. Perhaps the issue was in the actual hitch ball mount, that it was too high. So, after confirming with the tow dolly manufacturer the lowest that I could set the hitch and still garner their support, I purchased a new lower hitch ball mount. But, after trying to load the Civic with the new ball mount it would still not work.

I was at a loss. The tow dolly we purchased was not returnable. Even if I could return it, there was no other dolly that we could store. I considered modifying the dolly, but there were multiple problems with that approach. Not only would such modifications void the manufacturer's warranty, but I had neither the tools nor the expertise to do the work, nor did I know anyone else who could.

The least complicated option that we could come up with was to buy another car. Even though Lana loved her little Civic, she was willing to part with it if it meant that we could make a winter trip. So, she set about researching cars that had sufficient clearance to fit onto our tow dolly.

All I could think of was that this was getting complicated. We had already tied up a pretty good amount on the tow dolly. Now we were about to buy another car under pressure; not a comfortable position to be in, but what else could we do?

One day, in the midst of this mess our youngest son dropped by the house. He is very mechanically minded and very creative. We often discuss our projects and technical challenges. As we chatted I told him about the problem in loading Lana's car onto the dolly. We went out to the garage to look at the dolly as we talked. With little thought he suggested that I bolt a platform on top of the dolly to hold the car's wheels, raising them up enough to fit onto the dolly. Brilliant! Why had I not thought of that?

After a quick trip to the local home improvement store, I had all of the materials necessary to build a platform and attach it to the dolly in such a way as to not actually modify the dolly (*no holes, no welding, etc.*), thus not voiding the warranty. After a few hours of work, I had a platform built and mounted. It was ready for the big test.

I brought the bus home once again and hooked the dolly up. Lana eased her car up the ramps, as I guided her with my fingers crossed and a prayer in my mind. Closer and closer. Then the car settled onto the platform with a couple of inches to spare. It fit! We secured the car and took the bus and car for a test spin. It worked like a charm.

Once again, a seemingly insurmountable problem had been overcome. I had very little to do with the solution: all I provided were the hands and tools. Our winter trip had been saved in a manner I could have never foreseen, giving my bride a most welcome respite from the cold weather and us both shared memories of an adventure together. God's grace had, once again been shown to his children.

PSSSST

Winters in northern Ohio can come on quickly and with a vengeance. Since our plan was to leave on our winter trip in late December, we stored our bus in an indoor heated facility. This protected the bus from the elements and allowed us to leave the bus's power converter plugged in which kept the batteries fully charged. We planned to retrieve the bus the day before our planned departure, check it over and load it up, departing the next morning.

The afternoon before we planned to leave, we went to retrieve the bus. Since it was a cold day, I wanted to warm the inside of the bus up with the propane furnaces before I started driving. When I stored the bus, I had shut off the propane. So, as I opened the main service valve on the propane tank, I felt a cold blast on the back of my fingers and heard a little "psssst" sound. Then I sensed the distinct smell of propane. This was not right. So, I closed the valve. What now? I would think of a plan as I drove.

I had heard enough horror stories from my father-in-law about gas leaks that I knew I should not take any chances. On a winter trip we would certainly need the propane furnaces. But, with a propane leak we would not be able to run them. This would make for a very cold and uncomfortable trip. This would also prevent our use of the refrigerator and the water heater while we drove for four days. But. Most of all, a propane leak would make just being in the bus dangerous – way too dangerous.

As I drove the bus toward home I could see in my mind the piles of things stacked around the house ready to put on the bus. I could hear Lana's excited comments about the upcoming trip and how she was looking forward to spending a winter out of the cold. All of this was crashing down around me. If this propane leak could not be fixed and soon there would be no trip.

I recalled seeing a large propane company along one route home. So, I detoured and headed for what I hoped would be help. I explained my problem to the service manager, and was told that they could, indeed replace the failed valve. I was cautiously optimistic. This was great, but it wasn't fixed yet.

I pulled the bus around to the service area. I was met by a very friendly service technician. After I explained the problem to him, he said that they could replace the faulty valve, but the tank would have to be empty. Unfortunately, the tank was full. As luck would have it, I had filled the tank in the fall before storing the bus, thinking it would save us some time as we prepared to leave in December.

Not knowing what else to do, I headed for home with the bus. I wasn't sure how I was going to safely bleed off 20 gallons of propane in time to get the valve replaced by the end of the day. Nor was I looking forward to telling Lana that our trip was in jeopardy.

When I arrived at home, we discussed the problem and the very real possibility that we would not be able to make the trip. We were both heartbroken, but Lana took it better than I did; I felt that I had failed. Lana suggested that she call the bus's builder to see if he had any ideas on how to quickly drain the propane tank. I did not see how he could possibly help, but she insisted. When she got him on the phone, she brought the phone to me and insisted that I talk to him. I explained the problem. True to his nature, the builder had included into the propane manifold a separate bleed line for just such an eventuality. After a brief chat, and a couple of minutes with a wrench, I had the tank bleeding off propane. Well, alright then. Now we're getting somewhere.

As one might expect for a December day in northern Ohio, it was cold, which certainly did not speed along the flow of propane. After about 30 minutes, the end of the bleed line began to freeze up blocking the flow of propane. With effort I was able to keep this open most of the time. But, with the cold temperature not all of the propane would drain off: several gallons remained in a liquid state and remained in the tank. The propane service guy would not work on the tank unless it was completely empty.

While I worked to drain the propane out of the tank, I noticed liquid propane dripping from both of the regulators on the propane manifold. Yet another problem. Replacing a regulator is not a big deal. But replacing two would be no fun, especially out in the cold and literally working the street. Plus, I had no idea where I could buy replacement regulators in town.

This problem seemed to be going from bad to worse. The prospects for making this winter trip seemed to be growing ever dimmer.

On a whim I called a large RV and camping supply dealer on the other side of town. They said that they had the regulators in stock, could would be glad to do the work, and actually had time that day to do it. I was in the bus headed that way almost before I could hang up the phone. They took the bus right back into their shop, and in a couple of hours both of the regulators had been replaced. As I chatted with the guy at the service desk, I explained the problem with the faulty valve, and that I had to drain the tank completely before I could get the valve replaced. They were kind enough to keep the bus inside their heated service area for a couple more hours, allowing the propane to warm up. They then parked it in their parking lot and finished draining off the propane. They then removed the faulty valve fitting just to make sure that there was no residual pressure in the tank. After which they replaced the valve tightening it only hand-tight, knowing that it would be removed and replaced soon.

I could almost see the light at the end of the tunnel. All I needed to do now was to get the propane company to replace the valve and we were good to go. I called them to make sure they would still be open when I got there. Sure enough they would be, so I headed that way. The light at the end of the tunnel was getting brighter.

IT'S NOT MY FAULT

After what seemed like an eternity, I arrived back at the propane company to have the faulty propane valve replaced. Once again I explained the problem to the folks at the service desk. They directed me to move the bus to the service area: a service technician would be there momentarily. However, instead of the kind service technician I had encountered on my first visit, a young man with an attitude came to meet me. As I explained the problem and what I needed, he kept saying that they don't work on RV's and wondered why the front desk had sent me back to him. Through all of his grousing, I finally convinced him to replace the valve in our tank: I didn't need anyone to "work on an RV".

As he begrudgingly got to work, I walked around the service yard, pondering the events of the past several hours, and beginning to feel relief that I was nearing the end of yet another bus challenge. After a few minutes he called out that he was done. I explained to him that I now needed to fill the tank. Then he started mumbling that "it wasn't my fault", that "it was already broken", and "the valve should have never been loosened". I was puzzled: what in the world was this guy talking about? Then I looked at the tank and the new valve.

What I saw shocked me. He had replaced the valve, alright. But, in the process he had destroyed the copper line that feeds propane from the tank into the distribution manifold. It seems that he grabbed a wrench and started cranking on the valve without removing the copper line, or even checking to see if the valve was already loose. All I got from him was that it wasn't his fault: he didn't break it. But it was broken nonetheless.

Since the faulty valve had been replaced, it was safe to put propane in the tank once again, which he did. At least I had a full tank and it wasn't leaking. But with the destroyed copper line, it we had no way to actually get the gas to the furnaces or anything else. It was still useless.

A quick trip to the office yield nothing but a receipt marked "paid". I hoped to at least get a suggestion as to where I might be able to have another copper line made.

Another customer suggested a local truck garage: he felt sure that they had the necessary tools to flange copper tubing. Having nothing to lose, off I went.

As I drove I became increasingly disappointed. Through all of this, I had gotten so close to getting the problem fixed and being on the way to a warm winter for Lana. But, now, once again I had no idea how I could possibly get this fixed. I was running out of both time and ideas. All I could think of was an old saying from my flying days: "Never run out of airspeed, altitude and options at the same time". I felt that was exactly what had happened to me.

I finally found the little truck garage. When I explained my problem and what I needed, the folks there looked at me like I had two heads. Needless to say they were no help.

I was really depressed now. The trip that Lana wanted - no, "needed" – so badly was gone. There had been a light at the end of the tunnel, but I discovered that it was a train headed right for me and I wasn't able to get off of the tracks in time.

The drive home from the propane company was a sad and lonely drive, even though it was only a few miles. I pondered the recent events and racked my brain for an idea as to where I could have the part I needed made. But I came up empty.

As I neared home I recall my praying through the tears, truly laying this at the foot of the cross. I told God that I had done all I could do, and that if this trip were meant to happen it would be completely up to him. Through my many years of following Jesus, I had heard people talk about complete surrender. This was a moment of complete surrender for me.

As I drove through one of the many roundabouts near our house, the name of a small plumbing supply shop came to mind. Instead of passing through the round-about, I took the first exit and started toward that shop. It was not my idea. I was not really familiar with what they carried, or even if they would be open that hour of the day. But away I went.

After I managed to park the bus in their little parking lot, I went in and explained my problem to the lady behind the counter. I hoped that she would either be able to make the tube I needed or, at least recommend someone who could. She vanished around a corner and down an aisle, reappearing a few seconds later with a stainless steel tube. She explained that these were now commonly used in place of copper, but that this was the only one she had.

I had the broken-off end of the original tube in my hand, which we carefully compared to the stainless steel tube. The fittings were a perfect match. A quick measurement revealed that it was exactly the right length. With tears in my eyes I explained the recent events to the lady and paid her. I literally ran out to the bus, grabbed a wrench and removed the rest of the old tube. The new stainless steel tube was a perfect fit. A few cranks with the wrench, and I had a fully functional, brand new propane gas distribution system on the bus. Warm weather here we come!

I have had many conversations with my brothers in Christ over the years about what it means to completely surrender yourself to God. Though some of the discussions have been very lively, I do not recall anyone ever truly defining exactly what complete surrender means.

Through the ages men have fought battles and wars. As horrible as war is, it brings out very basic and fundamental elements of mankind. Men have been known to do incredible, seemingly impossible things in the heat of battle. War also elicits very basic and extreme emotions from the combatants as well as all of those who are affected by the conflict. The very last act of an army that has no options left, no hope of defeating the opposing force is surrender. If the defeat has been complete, the army is forced into an unconditional surrender, where the defeated army has no say in what comes next. Such a surrender is a very fundamental and basic act: an act of desperation.

I think this is exactly what complete surrender to God means: knowing that you have no other option and will have no say in what happens next. This sounds ominous, until we realize that we are surrendering to a God, a father who loves us more than words can express, who is waiting for us to climb into his lap and let him love us. It is in this context that we give up control and throw in the towel.

This is exactly what happened to me on the road to the plumbing supply shop that day. I had been completely overwhelmed by the circumstances, and had exhausted all of my options. I had no cards left to play. But I knew that God loved Lana and me and only wanted the best for us. If he would have us to make this winter trip and for Lana to avoid yet another painful winter, then it would have to be up to him because I could no longer influence the outcome. I raised the white flag of surrender in a very real sense that afternoon. As I drove home from the plumbing shop, I knew that I was not in control, and that brought a deep sense of peace.

ON THE ROAD AGAIN

After what seemed an interminable period of minor repairs and difficulties and planning we finally setoff for our winter retreat. The weather was mild for a northern Ohio December, forecast to remain above freezing for our entire trip. The bus was packed and the tow dolly carrying our little Honda Civic rolling merrily along behind us. All that was ahead of us was about 32 hours of driving in increasingly warm weather.

Being the first time we had pulled a trailer of any type behind the bus, I was a bit apprehensive. Since I had made a bolt-on modification to the tow dolly in order to accommodate our car, I was keenly aware of all of the things that could go wrong. OK. Like many of you I, too am a worrier about some things. And I was a bit worried about safely making this trip with so many variables in play. But, the first two days proved to be uneventful.

THAR SHE BLOWS!

As we readied the bus for our third day, I noticed that it was pretty windy. But, we had 40,000 pounds of bus under us. We weren't in some lightly constructed motorhome with plastic walls. It would be fine. What could possibly go wrong?

So, coffee in hand, and bus fired up, we pulled onto the freeway. I felt the wind pushing us around a bit, but it certainly posed no threat or concern. Then, after only a few minutes on the road I happened to catch a glimpse of something in my side mirror. I looked but didn't see anything and kept on driving. Then, I saw it again. It was the awning over the bedroom window: the wind had blown it open and it was ferociously flapping in the wind.

I knew that I had to stop and quickly or the awning would be torn from the bus. There just happened to be an exit where we were, leading to a side access road. Fortunately, being in the middle of nowhere there was little traffic on the access road. So, onto the access road we pulled and brought the bus to a stop.

I grabbed a small step ladder from the cargo bay, and took a close look at the awning. It didn't appear to be damaged, but given the wind, damage would almost certainly come if I couldn't get it secured. Being the designated bus mechanic it was my job to fix the problem and get us back on our way. But, I had no clue how I could secure the awning.

We keep a small toolbox on the bus, along with duct tape and some other essential repair materials and tools. But, given that space is limited, so are the tools and supplies. So, standing on that step ladder trying to keep from being blown off, maybe 20 feet from a busy freeway with cars and trucks buzzing by, I racked my brain as to how to secure the awning, but all I received was a test pattern and monotone audio signal (*Yes, I do remember these on the TV late at night "back in the day"*). In short, I was coming up empty.

I don't recall any specific prayer, but prayer for bus problems had become almost reflexive by this time, so I am sure that I spoke with God about it, albeit briefly.

Back to the toolbox I went, just to see if something came to mind. I felt like our oldest son when he was a teenager: he could stand in front of an open refrigerator for what seemed like hours, close it and leave empty handed, only to return a few minutes later. When asked why he returned, he would reply, "I thought I might see something I missed". Yeah, that was exactly what I was doing. I was hoping that I might just see something that would trigger an idea as to how to resolve our problem.

Then I noticed our little battery-powered drill. Not too powerful, but it had come in handy. What else ... what else? Then I noticed a big bag of zip ties. For the un-indoctrinated, zip ties are no doubt a gift from Heaven. They are small, cheap, secure and strong enough to hold just about anything you can wrap one around.

So, back up the ladder I went, drill in hand and with a pocket full of zip ties. A good start, but I had no clue what I could run the zip ties through on the bus to secure the awning. Then I noticed a small mounting rail that runs the length of the bus where the awnings mount to the bus. There was just enough of a lip on the rail to make drilling a small hole possible without damaging anything else. I drilled one hole and wrestled a zip tie into it and around a portion of the awning. It looked like it would work! So, I went all around the bus, drilling the same hole and putting a zip tie on each awning arm, securing all of the awnings. At least, I hoped it would secure them.

After storing all of my stuff, we pulled back onto the freeway, fingers crossed. After several pretty strong gusts of wind, the awnings held firmly. Problem solved!

As a footnote: in the months since this windy experience, I have noticed several other RVs and motorhomes with zip tied awnings. Great ideas are hard to keep down.

TOO CLOSE FOR COMFORT

With 2,200 and three days miles behind us, we neared our winter destination. I had kept a keen eye on the tow dolly and our little Honda Civic. I guess that I expected to see it all collapse into a pile of wreckage, or turn into a fireball, but it hadn't. I checked the dolly and car whenever we would stop, and kept the mounting straps tight on the front wheels. It looked as though my bolt-on addition had worked beautifully.

Finally, we exited the freeway. Just a mile or so to go. Man, was I ready to get somewhere, ANY-where. Finally, here we were. I eased the bus into the driveway of the park, set the parking brake and shut the bus down. We had made it. As we were talking with the park staff getting checked in, another guest drove in, and commented to the park staff: "There is a big chunk of metal and wood in the driveway. Someone should move it before a car gets damaged." I thought nothing of it.

After a bit, we were directed to the site where we would spend the winter. So, I got busy unhooking everything, and getting ready to remove the car from the tow dolly. As I removed the wheel straps, I noticed that a large metal piece that was part of my bolt-on addition and a large section of the wooden platform were gone. Not broken or bent, but GONE. Then it hit me: I wonder if this was what the other park guest was talking about in the driveway. So, I hoofed it back to the entrance, and there was the missing piece of our tow dolly platform. As well as I could figure, the straps were not quite tight enough, and the turn into the park driveway – which was a bit bumpy and abrupt – caused car to shift slightly breaking the board away, sending it and the metal piece bolted to it into the driveway . . . about 100 feet from our ultimate destination.

We had made it safely, but I must admit that I lost more than a little sleep thinking about what might have happened had the tow dolly failed while we were zooming down the highway.

TOW DOLLY 2.0

As I mentioned earlier, the tow dolly required modifications before our car would fit. This modification had worked, getting us and our car safely to our destination - almost. But, the modification failed in the last few feet. We had made it safely, as had our car. But . . . how in the world were we going to get the car home? I had tried the best idea available with the first modification, and it had failed. Even if I could come up with a better design, I didn't have the tools I would need or the place to work. In a strange city, I didn't even know who I might hire to do the work. You see, one thing about a converted bus is that it is 100% custom. You generally can't run down to the "dealer" to buy a part or get something fixed. Our jerry-rigged tow dolly was no different. I would have to come up with a plan myself. No pressure. We would simply be stuck there until I figured it out. Yep, more sleepless nights.

I am like many guys I know in that I tend to solve problems in my sleep or in the shower. And, let me tell you, many was the night that I worked on that tow dolly in my sleep. After what seemed like months, I finally had an idea as to how I might design a better platform.

I would need another large chunk of wood – a big 2 x 12. I had used pressure treated pine the first time, but it had split. So, I needed something better. I looked in the home improvement and lumber places close to us, and found squat. And, even if I could find a suitable board, how could I fabricate it.

Then I recalled seeing something in the park brochure about a woodshop in the park that was available for guests to use in making various crafts. So, one morning I pedaled up to the woodshop on my trusty Schwinn. The shop was very well equipped, with all of the tools I would need to fabricate another platform. The guy in charge told me that a membership was required in order to use the shop or the tools. I thought, "Here it comes. It'll cost a zillion dollars". "$25 for the year", he told me. Seriously? I couldn't get $25 out of my pocket fast enough.

OK. One part of the problem was solved. But I still needed to find a suitable board. So, I asked the guy in the woodshop where I might find some hardwood boards big enough. He recommended a specialty lumber shop across town. They had just about every kind of wood you could imagine. So, I called them and asked what they had in a 2 x 12. I was told that they might have some that big, but I would just have to come and look through the piles myself. To make a long story short, I went, I dug, I found. But you should have seen me try to get a 50 pound 10 foot long 2 x 12 back to the bus in a little Honda Civic. I am surprised that I didn't get pulled over!

So, I had the board and the place and tools to fabricate it. But, the metal tire cradles I had designed needed to be made. So, I started looking for machine shops. Yep, you guessed it: zilch. I asked around and got no help. Without a shop to do the metal fabrication we were nowhere. Then, I happened to see an ad somewhere (*probably on one of the bulletin boards in the park's activities building*) for a place that made big metal lawn art. It was a long shot, but I thought it worth a try. So, I drove out into the desert and found this little place. I explained to one of the guys there my dilemma and asked if that was something they might be able to make for me. He said that he would need to see a drawing first, but he was pretty confident that they could come make them. Great!

I drew up a detailed drawing of the cradles I needed and delivered them to the metal fab shop. After a few delays and several weeks, I finally went to pick them up. I guess that my expectations were not very high. After all, these guys made metal lawn decorations. What did they know about tow dollies? But I had grossly underestimated these guys. They did a masterful job. The cradles were exactly what I had designed. Now, if they would only work.

Fast forward to the day of our departure in late March. The tow dolly platform had been fabricated and bolted into position, the two tire cradles had been fabricated and bolted into place, and the tow dolly was hitched to the bus. We were ready to roll . . . well, almost. We still had to load the car onto the dolly. The one final BIG test remained. But, the car snuggled into the cradles beautifully. So, with the car all secured onto the dolly, off we went. 2,200 miles later the car hadn't moved an inch; version 2.0 of my improvised tow dolly platform had worked great.

After we got everything unloaded and the bus stored, I had a chance to reflect over the events of the winter and on the events surrounding the tow dolly. Like so many prior instances with the bus, there were so many details that were so far beyond my capabilities, so many "coincidences", so many times when God's hand was clearly in the details. I thought many times how sad it was that I was actually surprised to find God's hand in so many details of this adventure. I should have expected to find the Creator of the universe in the midst of everything. But, yet it seemed strange to me that he would want to be involved in the efforts of an old man working to keep a 50 year old bus on the road. Were these things truly important to God?

COOKING ON THE BIG BURNER

The builder of our bus had done an incredible job of converting an old transport bus into a home on wheels. He had included almost everything one could imagine. During the years that he and his wife had driven around the country in the bus, he had added many things that he had not initially thought of. One of those things was a built-in, pull-out gas grill. All one need to do is to open a bay door, slide the grill out on its rack, turn a valve and throw on the burgers.

During our short time with the bus we had used the grill many times. Usually, I would fire it up, let it get to cooking temperature, throw on dinner, and go back inside or go about doing something else, somewhere else, returning occasionally to check on dinner.

One evening in early March during our first winter trip we decided to grill out. So, I did what I normally do: I pulled the grill out, fired it up, and went back inside to get dinner. But this time, after I put dinner on to cook, I pulled up a chair on the patio by the grill and just enjoyed the beautiful weather.

As I watched people walk by, and casually read a book, I only half-heartedly paid attention to the grill. I had done this many times. I knew about how long it would take to cook. So, I really didn't need to watch it very closely. But, then something caught my attention: the grill was making unusual sounds. Nothing huge, just different. But I nonchalantly pushed that tidbit of information to the back of my mind and went on with my book.

There it was again: an unusual sound. This time it was a bit louder, sounding a bit like a jet engine off in the distance. When I glanced at the grill, I saw flames shooting out from below the grill. Perhaps the wind was just blowing the flames from inside the grill, but perhaps I should take a closer look. As I leaned down to peek underneath the grill, I saw the problem. The rubber hose that feeds gas to the grill was ruptured just below the burner. It had caught fire and was burning like a blowtorch and burning away the hose, edging ever closer to the propane tank and regulators.

By the time I managed to reach around the flames and shut off the propane, the paint on the control panel on the front of the grill had bubbled up from the heat, with much of it having burned off. After I regained my composure, I realized just how close this had come to being an all-out disaster. I have seen gas grills malfunction before, and in one instance coming close to burning down a neighbor's house.

What "luck" that I had chosen to sit outside by the grill this particular afternoon. OK. You're right. I use the word "luck" tongue-in-cheek. There was no luck involved at all. I will always believe that God's hand was in this incident, just like all of the others. I can't say why, nor can I even say how. But, he managed to keep me there to catch and extinguish the fire. I still get goose bumps thinking about what could have happened.

A FEW "LITTLE" PROJECTS

I have often joked (*OK, not really joking*) that owning a 50 year old converted transport bus was like owning an old car and an old house all rolled into one. There was always something that needed to be repaired or refurbished. After having spent over three months living in the bus that winter, there were several things that popped up that would need to be repaired before we made another trip. Nothing big like an engine falling out, or a wheel coming off. Just fairly minor things, or at least so I thought.

Previous winters had not been kind to our plumbing. The main shutoff valve for the "shore" fresh water line was malfunctioning, several of the shutoff valves in the fresh water distribution manifolds were leaking, and there was a leak in the waste water manifold. Since we were living in the bus and needed fresh water, these were not projects that could realistically be tackled until we returned home. But, the complexity of each of these projects gnawed at me. How could I attack each problem? What materials would I need and where could I get them? How can I rebuild such major components, especially since I am certainly no plumber? But, the biggest concern I had was that any of these repairs failed, the bus would be unusable.

Professional help; that's what I needed. No, not psychiatric help, but help from a skilled craftsman. I needed a seriously talented plumber. But, what plumber in his/her right mind would agree to work on a 50 year old converted coach?

After we returned home for the summer, I contacted a plumber friend who had done work for us at home in the past. I explained the problems, and he said that he would be willing to take a look, but he was extremely busy. He wanted me to contact him as soon as his kids were out of school. Then he might have time.

So, a couple of months later I contacted him again. Not only had his schedule not improved, but he had gotten ever busier (*Yeah, I know – who ever heard of an underworked plumber?*). But he was still encouraging, and asked me to keep reminding him. So, every week or so I would text him to keep my project in front of him. Finally, in early July he hinted that there was no way on God's green earth that he would have time to work on our bus. Heavy sigh!

He was my only hope for a professional plumber. If he couldn't' make these repairs, then I was sunk. I couldn't do this stuff. I had no experience with high precision ABS fabrication or complex brass manifolds. So, back to the frequent sleepless nights.

After what seemed like months of pondering and worrying, I decided to try to eat this elephant myself, one bite at a time. I would try to replace the faulty shore water valve. This was the simplest of the repairs. Maybe, just maybe I could at least complete this one repair.

Contrary to my nature, I pondered the repair carefully, looking into the exact valve I needed, the exact process I should go through to replace it, what could possibly go wrong, and how to avoid each of these undesirable outcomes. I think the technical word for this state of mind is "patience".

After all of the planning and worrying, the day finally came. A quick trip to the plumbing supply shop, and a couple of hours with my head in the fresh water bay, the faulty valve had been replaced. Victory! Well, at least I had won the first battle. But the remainder of the war still loomed in front of me.

I savored my victory for a while, and concluded that if I managed to fix one of the problems it might just be possible for me to fix two. So, I tackled rebuilding both of the fresh water manifolds. I won't bore you with the details, but it was just like the first plumbing project. After a lot of planning and patience, and many trips to the plumbing supply shop, and a lot of time spent in the bus's fresh water bay and in my workshop, we had new fresh water manifolds with heavy duty brass globe valves.

OK. I had already accomplished WAY beyond what I knew how to do, and more than I ever expected. But I could not stop now. The leaky waste water manifold had to be rebuilt, and this project would be a doozy. It involved very an exacting design, precisely cutting and assembling a bunch of ABS pipe and fittings with three ABS gate valves, and installing them onto our two waste water tanks. The very tight tolerances were more like a high precision metal fab project. There was very little space in the bus for the manifold, plus the manifold had to line up perfectly with the outlet ports on the two waste water tanks. On top of this, the folks at the plumbing supply shop warned me that the ABS cement setup very quickly; once I put two pieces together, I would not be able to realign them; they had to be perfect from the outset.

Once again, I measured, I designed, I measured, I planned, I measured, I worried, I measured, I spoke with the folks at the plumbing supply shop, I measured. I did everything but begin to actually work on the manifold. I dreaded it. I was genuinely concerned that I would screw it up somehow, and disable the bus.

Again, fast forward. With help from a friend that has a lot of expensive tools, and a willingness to help, I finally had a completed manifold sitting in my workshop. Everything was the right size (*at least the size that I had intended it to be*). The real test would be fitting it into the bus and onto the waste water tanks. If there was the slightest problem, I would have to start all over: buying yet three more valves, and rebuilding the whole thing. I was a very reluctant amateur plumber to say the very least.

The day came when I could put off the inevitable no longer. After a bit of struggling, and a few minor last minute changes in my installation plans, I got it installed. It fit like a glove. The result was exactly what I had hoped for.

After catching my breath, and cleaning up my workshop, I reflected on these plumbing projects. These were so far beyond my skills and abilities as to be laughable. The implications of failure of any of these projects would have meant that the bus would be unusable. My usual harried approach to these problems would have led to almost certain failure. I had no explanation for the outcome but the hand of God. Once again his intervention saved the day. I recall being struck with awe realizing that God's love for us was so extreme that he would pay attention to and fix plumbing.

WHILE YOU'RE AT IT

The summer of the great plumbing projects brought other "opportunities" as well. There were some other equipment problems that needed attention.

The bus had a backup camera that is essential when backing the bus up. Age had not been kind to the old monitor. Whenever the temperature would drop below about 50°, the monitor would just roll, providing no clear picture at all, rendering it useless in cool or cold weather. After being told by the camera system's manufacturer that a replacement would cost almost $2,000, I decided to put this project off for a while.

The other problem involved the windshield wiper on the passenger side of the bus. The wipers are powered by the bus's compressed air system. The valve that operated the passenger side wiper was going bad, making its operation iffy and unpredictable. But, accessing the back of the valve inside of the dash would be very difficult if not outright impossible. Plus, any misstep in connecting the airlines could potentially render the bus inoperable (*unable to release the parking brake*). So, this problem, too was delayed indefinitely.

As summer set in and my mind turned to making bus repairs, I concluded that both of these projects might be doable if I did them both at the same time. Once I removed the old backup monitor, I should be able to reach the airlines and replace the wiper valve. But, I was not excited about spending $2,000 on a new camera and monitor. Plus, I had no clue where to buy pneumatic wiper valves.

Once again, patience and prayer were my primary tools. An alternate provider for a camera system almost literally fell into my lap. They could provide a replacement for less than $400. And, it was color and high resolution. A provider for the needed windshield wiper was likewise discovered.

The camera project was littered with more technical details and challenges than should be relayed here. But, one by one they were each resolved, allowing me to reuse the difficult components from the old system. A couple of weeks after first tearing into the dash and camera hood, we had a new HD color camera and monitor.

Along the way, the replacement wiper valve had been replaced, having been identified, purchased, shipped and installed in the course of about one week.

The thing that is most noteworthy to me about these issues is finding a camera system that was vastly superior over our old one at a fraction of the cost. Plus, had we not been able to re-use the wiring from the old camera system, I don't think it would have been possible to replace the old camera.

But, as with so many problems and challenges before, these somehow got worked out and brought to a successful conclusion.

DRIP, DRIP, DRIP

After all of the summer's projects had been completed, only one thing remained: to actually put water in all of the plumbing and check for leaks. I put this off as long as possible. Finally, I could delay no longer, unless we cancelled our planned winter trip. So, one week when the early fall weather was beautiful (*and not likely to be so for long*), I took the plunge figuratively.

With no water in the bus's fresh water tank, the first task was to un-store the bus and bring it to our house for the day. After taking care of a couple of other minor maintenance chores, I got down to work. The first task was to fill the waste water tanks to ensure that they would hold the pressure without leaking. Into the bus I went, garden hose in hand. Eventually, I had two full waste water tanks. With more than a little trepidation, I went down to the waste water bay and looked for the leaks I expected to find. But, the bay was dry. No leaks in sight, even after quite a while under pressure. Chalk this one up in the win column.

Next, I put water into the fresh water tank, and after saying a now all too familiar plumbing prayer, I flipped the switch to pump water into the newly rebuilt plumbing. As you might have guessed, water was leaking from everywhere. It seemed as though every joint was leaking. Not surprising, I guess but still it was way disappointing.

Like so many times before the proverbial clock was ticking. We were planning to leave for the winter in about one month. Without functional plumbing we would not be able to make the trip. As cold weather settled in, it would be impossible to work further on the plumbing. So, it was now or never.

With no other option, I once again (*seemingly for the zillionth time*) tore out the fresh water manifolds and headed to my workshop. I completely disassembled both manifolds and very carefully and laboriously reassembled them. The next day after I headed back to the bus. This would certainly be the last time I had to work on these bad boys. Surely I had all of the leaks fixed (*fingers crossed*).

The weather was still on my side, but, I knew it would not last. I carefully reinstalled the manifolds, said my plumbing prayer, and flipped the water pump switch. Yeah. You guessed it. Drip, drip, drip. There was still one leak. Not a bad one (*I guess there is really no such thing as a good leak*), but it would still have to be fixed before we could travel in the bus. And, there was no way on God's green earth that it could be fixed while the manifolds were installed in the bus.

Tick, tock, tick, tock . . .

So, out came the manifolds yet again. After a hurried workshop session I had, once again (*I hoped*) fixed the leak. But this time I devised a way to pressure test each manifold before I installed them in the bus. I had no desire to keep on installing and uninstalling these bad boys. Sure enough they were tight and dry. What could go wrong now? All I had to do was to reinstall them and connect the water lines in the bus. Piece of cake.

So, another beautiful fall morning found me on my knees with my head in the fresh water bay. After I got the cold water manifold in place, I turned on the water pump. And there was a small drip where one of the bus water lines connected to the manifold– about one drip every couple of seconds. Not a big deal, but we certainly couldn't live in the bus for four months with that leak. I removed the offending water line, hoping to see something obvious. Nothing. It looked OK to me. But, then again I am no plumber. What did I know?

The plumbing in our bus is fairly old. My guess is that it was part of the initial conversion in the late 1980's. Virtually every plumbing component was common in RV's of the day. Suffice it to say that parts for these pipe fittings and other small components are not common fare in most hardware and home improvement stores some 20 years later. Actually, I have never seen any of this stuff in any store or shop anywhere.

So, back to my leaky fitting. There is a compression washer that is supposed to keep such fittings from leaking. So, I pulled this washer off of the leaky water line. It looked a little chewed up, but I was certain that I would never be able to replace it. But, perhaps I could reshape and smooth it out enough to seal properly. Then, I thought of my buddy in the plumbing supply shop who had saved the day with my propane line the previous year. I would run down there, show her the part and see if she had any ideas on how to seal this puppy.

So, I stuffed the questionable washer into my jeans pocket and headed home before going to the plumbing shop. When I got home, Lana asked how things were going. I explained it all to her, and said that I was headed to the plumbing shop to see if they had any ideas. As I reached into my pocket to retrieve the bad washer to show Lana, I discovered to my horror it was missing. "Here we go again", I thought. The bus is unlivable without water, and I had just lost the part that I needed to show the folks at the plumbing supply shop. How in the world could I even hope for an alternative if I didn't even have the original to show? Plus, now I would not even be able to put it all back together again without the missing part.

Lana, being the great supporter she is, basically said "Let's go", and back to the bus we went to try to find the part. I was pretty sure it had popped out of my pocket when I retrieved the bus keys to lock it up as I left. But, the missing part was gray. The real clincher is that the storage lot we use is covered with gray gravel and ground up bits of old asphalt pavement. I had dropped things on this stuff before, and never found them. It's like the ground just swallows stuff up. But, having no choice, on we went.

When we arrived at the bus, I went to where I had been working. I wanted to unlock the fresh water bay to show Lana what we were looking for. But first, I took a quick look at the ground to make sure that my feet would not simply be covering up the part we were looking for. I hadn't even begun to look at the ground good, when Lana walked up and asked, "Is this the part?" She held out her hand, and, sure enough, there it was. She saw it almost as soon as she got out of the car.

What a relief. At least now I had something to show the lady at the plumbing supply shop. Hopefully she would have some idea as to how I might seal this fitting and stop the leak. So, to the plumbing supply shop I went. As soon as I walked in the door, she greeted me and asked if she could help. I held out the bad washer and asked her if she had any idea how I might seal this leaky fitting. She disappeared down an aisle, reappearing a moment later with a small part in her hand. "It's not exactly the same. I only have them in white." As I looked at the part, I realized that it was the exact same compression washer as the bad one. She even had replacements for the small metal retainer rings. Man, I didn't care if this thing was white, hot pink or any other color. So, not being one to pass on an opportunity, I bought six of them and six retainer rings (*for a grand total of $3.06*), and headed back to the bus.

As I drove I pondered the events of the day. Once again God had clearly intervened in a problem with our old bus. He had provided replacement parts for 30 year old plumbing that had long-since ceased to be widely used or manufactured. There was no other explanation. Lana finding the missing part under impossible conditions, the plumbing supply shop (*once again*) having the exact part I needed. For $3.06 the winter trip had been salvaged. I would call this anything but cheap grace.

WHOA BIG FELLA!

As the "summer of projects" drew to a close, we began to look forward to a return to a warm winter. All of the refurbishing and repair projects we had planned (*and some we had not planned*) were completed. Our old bus looked great, and all of the systems worked as they should. The only thing that remained was to have the mechanic shop take care of a few minor mechanical issues.

Over the course of the past year I would make a note of the things that needed attention. Before we dropped the buss off at the garage, I reviewed the list making sure that I had included everything. The items were relatively minor; things like changing the oil in the generator, and replacing the gasket on the radiator lid. As I prepared to print the list, I recalled that the bus seemed to take a little longer than usual to stop with the car in tow. So, it might be a good idea to have them at least check the brakes as long as it would already be in the shop. So, onto the list it went.

After the garage had a chance to look everything over, I heard from the service manager. He confirmed everything that we had asked them to look at. But, the brakes were a different story altogether.

There are six braking points on our bus. On each of these points is a gizmo called a "slack adjuster". This thing adjusts just how hard the brakes are actually applied when I step on the brake pedal. The range of adjustment runs from no braking at all to full-on "there's no way this bus is gonna move" braking. Of these six braking points, two had broken or faulty slack adjusters (*requiring replacement*) and the other four were way out of adjustment. It takes a lot of braking to stop a 40,000 pound vehicle rolling down the highway at 70 miles per hour. Here we had only 2/3 of our braking points functioning and they were barely functioning. In short, we were lucky to be able to stop at all. It was an outright miracle that we had not had a nasty accident as a result of this brake failure while we were towing the car, or any other time for that matter.

While the folks in the garage were checking out the brakes, they also found a broken stabilizer cylinder on the front suspension.

Yet, once again God was looking out for us and our old bus. I had not planned to have the brakes looked at; it was just a last minute addition to the list. Had I not just "happened" to add this to the list, our next trip might well not have ended pleasantly.

110 TO 20

Well, we were about 3 weeks away from leaving the frozen hinterlands for a warmer winter climate – WAY warmer. All of our refurbishing and repair projects had been finished. As soon as the mechanic shop finished with the brake repair (*and a few other minor mechanical things*) we would be all ready to go. The plan was to return the bus to the outdoor storage lot that we used, put a cover on it for the 3 weeks until we planned to leave.

Finally the service manager at the shop called to tell me that the bus was finished and ready for the road again. After I paid for the repairs and got a brief summary of the work performed, I thanked them for their help and headed out to the lot to start the bus up and drive it to the storage lot.

As I walked up to the bus door, I just happened to notice the right outer drive axle tire. It looked a little low to me. But, this was one of the hubs that the mechanic had to remove to replace the brake slack adjuster, so I wasn't overly concerned. But, I was in no rush and thought it best to check the pressure in all of the tires, especially that one. They all checked out just fine, showing about 110 lbs. of pressure each. But, the tire that caught my attention only had 20 lbs. or pressure!

I fired up our generator and turned on the auxiliary air compressor and inflated the tire to the desired 110 lbs. But I was concerned as to why it was so low. I didn't think the mechanic would have needed to deflate the tire to perform the work he had done, but I thought it best to go back into the shop and ask. Sure enough they had not messed with this tire at all, other than remove the wheel (*with the tire mounted and inflated*) and replaced it once they were done.

So, here I was, on the verge of a 5,000 mile round trip with a big question mark on one tire. If they hadn't messed with it, it "should" be OK. But, I did not relish the thought of being on the road in winter and having that tire go flat (*or worse*) in the middle of nowhere.

Almost before I had time to think it over, the service manager and the mechanic both suggested that I should have my tire guy look that tire over. But, I didn't have a "tire guy". I had not needed to purchase tires for the bus since we had owned it. I had no clue where to take it. But, almost before I had concluded that I had no clue where to go to have the tire looked at, the mechanic suggested a truck tire shop less than ¼ of a mile away. Well, I wasn't in a hurry, and having it looked at now would be way better than taking a chance.

So, I fired the bus up and went to the truck tire shop they suggested. As I walked into the door, the guy behind the counter asked how he could help me. I explained the problem, fully expecting to either have to come back or wait forever until they would have time to take a look. "Pull it on in and we'll take a look". Man! No waiting, no scheduling a time and coming back. They would get on it right now.

After about fifteen minutes the technician working on the tire came into the office and showed me what amounted to a damaged valve stem. It seems that when the folks at my mechanic shop had checked the bus over, they had checked all of the tires for proper inflation and had put some air into the troublesome tire. The valve core just happened to stick inside the damaged valve stem when they added air, causing the air to leak out and without them even noticing. The technician was sure that this was the problem.

So, another 10 minutes and $50 and I was on my way. As I had done many times before, I thought about this while I was driving the bus to the storage lot. The valve core just "happened" to stick at a time and place where the repair was convenient, quick, and cheap. I had just "happened" to notice the tire in the first place. Too many coincidences for them to be coincidences. Once again I felt God's hand on Lana and me and our old bus.

CHAPTER 7

GRACE INDEED

I was blessed to have been raised by wonderful Christian parents who instilled in me a knowledge of and a desire to know Jesus. Some of my fondest memories as a kid revolve around our church. As an adult, worship has always been an important part of my life. As a husband and father, it was important to me that we all, as a family worship and made church an important part of our lives. I knew all about Jesus.

But, it was not until I was in college that I accepted Jesus as my Savior. I will never forget the two guys from a local Baptist church who knocked on my door one afternoon. They explained in a simple and clear manner that knowing "about" Jesus was of little importance; truly knowing him was what really mattered, and the first step was to ask him into my life. After a couple of days thinking about this conversation, I did just that.

My salvation experience was not dramatic like some people have experienced. It is perhaps best described as a "start". That night I began to know, truly know Jesus.

At the age of 41 I attended a very special weekend with about fifty other men. During the course of that weekend, I began to understand that God loves me, warts and all, more than I could ever fully comprehend. As someone told me that weekend, "If you were the only person in the world, Jesus would have still come and died on that cross for you". Even though I had grown up in a loving family and was blessed to have an awesome and loving wife and children and extended family who loved me, I had never encountered such love as I was told that God had for me. How could it be that God loves a knucklehead like me?

Years later, as I struggled to understand why God had taken my little girl from me, I was more confused than ever. I knew that God loved me, but how could such a senseless loss figure into that love. As I watched my bride struggle with Keri's death in her own way, and being absolutely unable to help her, the reality of God's love began to fade into gray. I don't think my faith ever faltered, but I felt like I was in a little snow globe, and God had picked it up and shaken the daylights out of it. All I could do was to wait until the snowstorm subsided.

Then came the bus. Our old bus brought my bride pleasure and real joy when I was sure that such was no longer possible for her. This old bus gave me a sense of actually doing something to help Lana. More importantly it allowed her (*and me*) to make new memories with no connection to the unfathomable loss of our precious daughter. Our focus was turned forward rather than backward. We have had a lot of fun and made wonderful memories in our old bus. In this old bus we found something that we could do and enjoy together. We had truly begun to move forward.

Over the years we have had our bus, and through the many trips and countless hours of bumping down the road and talking, I have heard Lana say "I love the bus" more times than I could possibly recall, almost a daily comment. It has become clear to me just how much our bus has helped her. It has, likewise become clear that God was in the middle of this whole thing. He had used a 50 year old bus to restore his daughter and her helpless husband, showering them both in his boundless grace. There were no lightning bolts, no parted oceans, no fiery chariots; but it was a miracle nonetheless. And God's tool of choice was an old bus. As unlikely an instrument as I recall reading anywhere in Scripture.

I remain amazed that something as out of the ordinary as a half-century old bus has played a significant role in our lives, in helping us to move beyond the unimaginable pain of losing our daughter. The fact that God played a role in this restoration should be no surprise since a gap that wide could only be bridged with his help. However, his tool of choice is not what one would expect. Buying an old bus had never entered my mind. It was never even the remotest possibility. I am sure that this would not be the first suggestion out of anyone's mouth for a similar situation. But, I am convinced that this old bus was, in fact God's idea, born of his love for us, his children – his hurting and broken children.

God had not sent us to just any old bus. He sent us to the perfect bus for us. One that was well suited to us and the way we live. There were no major modifications necessary: no bunks to remove, no major appliances to purchase, no major equipment to add. I needed no special knowledge to be able to drive and operate our home on wheels. It fit us. Although we did some restoration and cleanup, all we really had to do was get in it and enjoy it. It was like our bus was ready made for us, it just took a while for it to find us.

As I look back across our bus experience and can begin to put into perspective the healing effect it has had on Lana and on me, it all seems so clear. God used the unlikely, almost laughable approach of an old bus. He intervened in so many ways in so many details, keeping the bus running and livable and safe. But, his choice of which bus, I believe was no random matter. Of all of the buses we might have bought, of all of the people we might have dealt with, he put Ed and Anke in our path.

Ed's incredible attention to detail created a bus that fit our needs perfectly, even though we didn't even know what our needs were. On many occasions he has answered emails or phone calls from us inquiring about little details of our bus or buses in general, or even about RV-ing in general.

Ed and I have much in common. We are both engineers by degree and profession, both pilots, and both compulsive tinkerers. We can relate to each other in ways that most people can't. We both enjoy seeing a good design well executed, and basking in the glow of a job well done. These things have helped me to be able to draw on his experience and wisdom in many aspects of our bus adventure. I firmly believe that without Ed and "his" bus, we would have never been able to do this whole bus-thing. God did, indeed pick the perfect guy for us to work with and learn from.

Reflecting on the many, many instances when I was at my wit's end with the bus, and had no clue what to do much less how to do it, I can clearly see God's hand in each and every instance. Plus, he had put so many capable and willing people in our path to help keep our bus safely on the road. Any one of these things might be dismissed as coincidence or good luck. But, when taken in their entirety, it is (*as my Dad would say*) as plain as the nose on your face that God was in the middle of it, that it was his grace and love that found the missing set screw, and found the replacement propane gas line, and on and on.

Being unquestionably unqualified to maintain our bus and keep it on the road so Lana could enjoy it, I had no choice but to rely on someone besides myself. In many ways, my only option was an unqualified trust in God. Perhaps for the first time in my life I was absolutely dependent upon God and his grace and mercy. There was nothing that I could do on my own to affect the outcome of our bus experience.

I am still amazed that God chose to intervene in our lives as he did. He knew we both needed to move on after losing our daughter, but we didn't know how to do so. Using the characteristically unusual tool of an old bus, the perfect bus for us, the ideal builder, seller and friend to help us, and the countless times that his hands guided me in resolving problems and kept us safe, he set us both on the path to restoration.

The depth of God's love for his children has come into sharp focus for me through this experience. While we never know exactly how God will respond to a need, or what his answer will be to a prayer, we can rely absolutely on his unfailing love for his children; for you and me. If he was willing to use an old bus and a bumbling, unqualified shade-tree mechanic to restore one of his children, how can we ever doubt the depth of his love?

We had done nothing to deserve God's help, the bus, or anything else. We had simply suffered an unimaginable loss, but no one owed us anything. We had no right to expect anything. But here it came anyway: God's unmerited favor. He did for us what we did not deserve nor could expect. He helped two hurting parents to move ahead in a way that no one could have possibly imagined, and in probably the only way that would truly accomplish the healing that he intended.

We all have this love available to us. All we need to do is ask and God will shower us with love beyond our wildest expectations and in ways we cannot possibly imagine. Most of the time his response is not what I expect, but that is because of my limitations, not his. He always provides what I need, even if I don't realize it and certainly in spite of the fact that I don't deserve it.

God's unmerited favor. Grace, indeed.

"[...] may you have the power to understand, as all God's people should, how wide, how long, how high, and how deep his love is." Ephesians 3:18 (NLT)

EPILOGUE

Yes sir, our bus adventure has been an exceptional ride – figuratively and literally. It has seen my bride regain happiness and a general return to an active life. It has seen me begin the process of learning patience, plus a very real sense of having helped Lana in some small way rather than just standing around and watching her suffer.

But, perhaps more than anything else, it has shown me in a very clear and simple way that no detail is too small for God. I have also seen firsthand how God uses the unexpected and unusual for his purposes – and what could be more unusual than a half-century old bus and a helpless shade-tree mechanic?

There have been so many instances where I have unmistakably seen his hand through this experience that I am sure that I have overlooked some here. And I have also seen that there is no end to such instances of God demonstrating his love and grace through this old bus. If I had waited for a noticeable end to his involvement in our bus to begin to write, this book would have never been started. Even as the finishing touches are put on the publishing details, I continue to see God show us his grace through yet more instances of otherwise unexplainable results. I have no doubt that we will continue to see his grace in our lives through this bus and otherwise, if we will only look.

But the point is not details about our bus. Nor is it really about Lana or me. It is all about our loving Creator and his willingness – no, his desire – to shower his children with his love and his grace in ways that puts them in a state of awe. Sadly, it took this hardheaded author a while to recognize his hand and his grace.

It is my earnest prayer that you will take the time to turn around and look for his grace in your past, and grow to expect it in your future.

Made in the USA
San Bernardino, CA
19 December 2017